A Crisis of
Belief, Ethics, and Faith

Jonathan Finch

University Press of America,® Inc.
Lanham • Boulder • New York • Toronto • Plymouth, UK

Copyright © 2016 by University Press of America,® Inc.
4501 Forbes Boulevard, Suite 200, Lanham, Maryland 20706
UPA Acquisitions Department (301) 459-3366

Unit A, Whitacre Mews, 26-34 Stannary Street,
London SE11 4AB, United Kingdom

All rights reserved
Printed in the United States of America
British Library Cataloguing in Publication Information Available

Library of Congress Control Number: 2015948935
ISBN: 978-0-7618-6664-0 (pbk : alk. paper)—ISBN: 978-0-7618-6665-7 (electronic)

∞™ The paper used in this publication meets the minimum requirements of American National Standard for Information Sciences Permanence of Paper for Printed Library Materials, ANSI/NISO Z39.48-1992.

For my late father,
David Finch,
and the thinker in all of us.

Contents

Preface: A Crisis of Belief   vii

Acknowledgments   ix

I: The Foundations of Belief   **1**
  1. The Foundation of Thought: Self-Awareness   1
  2. The First Device: Observation   3
  3. The Second Device: A Bit of Logic   6
  4. Summary: Justified Beliefs   10

II: Explanations   **13**
  5. The Three Judges   13
  6. The Jigsaw Sphere: A Metaphor for Thought   16
  7. Two Kinds of Things: Thinking about Body and Mind   19
  8. On the Freedom of the Will   25
  9. Summary: Alligators and Ladders   27

III: The Search for Ethics   **29**
  10. Ethical Realism: The Search for Ethical Facts   29
  11. Non-Realist Ethics: The Search for Ethical Judgment   33
  12. Converting a Little Bit of Aristotle   37
  13. Converting a Little Bit of Kant   42
  14. Converting a Little Bit of Mill   43
  15. Putting All Three Together   45
  16. Summary: A Guide Book   50

IV: Political Economic Belief   **53**
  17. Moral Minimums and Deep Values   53

18. Closed Societies and Hierarchies	55
19. Some Suggestions in Political Economic Thought	57

V: Conclusion: From Faith to Philosophy — 59

20. Self-Mapping Robots	59
21. The Problem with Faith: The Metaphor of the Library	63
22. The Start of a Theology: TWIGTI	66
23. Epilogue: My Journey from Faith to Philosophy	71

Bibliography	75
Part One	76
Part Two	77
Part Three	77
Part Four	77
Part Five	78

Preface

A Crisis of Belief

When I was younger my mother would remark how I was such a nice boy. But around twelve years old, I started getting more and more angry. I was angry because I felt betrayed, betrayed by what I had been taught. My mother and her mother were both deeply Christian and fundamentalist in bent of thought but were also well educated. I was thus raised to think and question but also to accept Christian conclusions as the correct result of this process.

I later learned that the age of twelve is when children stop relying heavily on absorption when learning and start thinking critically, forming their own ideas. I had taken to biblical study in those early years, as much from an interest as self-defense, and had started to find problems with a fundamentalist reading of the Bible and Christian thought in general. I don't remember a particular day when I put it all together enough to reject these teachings, but I do remember periods of increasing difficulty with accepting what was being said and taught. During high school I was increasingly forced to attend church against my will, and when I left for college I ended all contact with organized religious ceremonies except for visits home.

My crisis in belief then really starts, in terms of altering my thought and behavior, around age 12 and has continued until almost my 40th birthday. In college and graduate school, I had the chance to study philosophy, which introduced me to all kinds of intellectual options in terms of why to believe and what to believe. Vital information for deciding how to understand and define myself and what kind of person I wanted to try and become. Philosophy gave me the options that my childhood education had missed, and to this day it remains a great deal of fun to do as well. My crisis in belief was a troubling matter, and I hope in the coming pages, in whole or in part, to assist others with similar concerns.

Acknowledgments

In December of 1999 I moved to Prague, the capital city of the Czech Republic. A month later, in January of 2000 I went to work for a private university, the University of New York in Prague, teaching philosophy in English. Soon thereafter I also started teaching philosophy online with Columbia College out of Missouri in the United States. Between these two jobs I was able to stay in or around Prague for next seven years, until early January of 2008. Overall my time in Prague was an irreplaceable experience in terms of study and thinking. If you spend your entire life in one society it is easy to miss, and hence never question, any number of cultural assumptions. The Czech people are thus to be thanked for their irreplaceable beer, some very enjoyable times and their hospitality. My stay there has had some real influence on my thoughts.

There are others to thank as well. My parents and my maternal grandmother have a great deal to do with the quality of my education and ensuring that I received one. My teachers and students, of course, have played a tremendous role in shaping and helping me to express my thoughts. I have bothered all sorts of people, family, friends and sometimes strangers as well, in my efforts to sort out my thoughts on this matter and they are to be thanked as well.

Dakota Fletcher and Bryce Schumacher, two of my students in particular made some very helpful comments. Tim Childers and Joel Dittmer, two philosophy professors, are also to be thanked for their contributions. Tim needs to be thanked for discussing these and other themes with me when I was in Prague, Joel for a review of an earlier draft of this work. Phil Boeckman and Bob Norton, two attorneys and two of the sharpest minds one is likely to meet, have both made some very important comments, criticisms, and suggestions that really helped in finishing this material.

Lynn Weber is owed a great deal of thanks for editing this document, easing the flow of discourse and cutting down on the redundancies. I, of course, take full responsibility for any of the remaining errors as I made the final determinations on the appearance of this material.

My sister, Lucy Finch, is to be thanked for providing the picture for the cover. It is a testimony to her rural skills that I did not know she was behind me when she took it. When one grows up a family farm in the middle of Missouri, one creates one's own games. Lucy and I took some pride in our ability to move very quietly and to detect others sneaking up on us; she won this round.

I

The Foundations of Belief

1. THE FOUNDATION OF THOUGHT: SELF-AWARENESS

When one starts doubting his or her beliefs, thinking one's beliefs to be mistaken; looking for something certain, something that escapes doubt, is a good starting point. Certainty dispels doubt and if something certain can be found it might provide a basis by which one might construct other beliefs and explanations. Beliefs, among other things, serve as platforms of action; when one is in doubt, going forward with confidence is nearly impossible. If doubt is extreme it can even cripple action.

It would be nice to have a reliable method of reducing this doubt and it is here that we can borrow our first lesson from philosophy and Rene Descartes, a seventeenth-century scientist and philosopher. Descartes had undergone a crisis in belief and decided to try and rebuild his thoughts from an infallible foundation; as he notes in the beginning of his book *Meditations on First Philosophy*,

> Some years ago I was struck by the large number of falsehoods that I had accepted as true in my childhood, and by the highly doubtful nature of the whole edifice that I had subsequently based upon them. I realized that it was necessary, once in my life, to demolish everything completely and start again from the foundations if I wanted to establish anything...that was stable and likely to last...

His search for something "stable and likely to last" led him through a series of hypotheses about what could be known for sure. After running through the possibilities, he found that there is only one thing he can be certain of, his own existence. He realizes he cannot rely on the reality of what he perceives through his senses, what he thinks he knows about the world. That world might be a dream or an illusion; his senses might mislead him. He *must* doubt them.

Descartes realized the ability to doubt proves the reality of the doubter. How could one have doubts and there not be something that does the doubting? He might be wrong about the world, but he could not be wrong about his awareness of his own thoughts and therefore could be certain of his own mental existence. From this conclusion comes his famous and often quoted "I think therefore I am." This is the foundation upon which Descartes begins to rebuild his thinking. The one thing he finds he can be certain of is his own existence.

Saint Augustine, a fifth-century North African philosopher, touched on these same issues many centuries earlier. In *The City of God* he asserted, "For he who is not, cannot be deceived: and if I am deceived, by this same token I am." In this statement he shares with Descartes the insight that our awareness of our own thoughts proves that these thoughts are real, that they exist. Therefore, the individual with self-awareness can know that they have some sort of mental existence.

I discuss Descartes and Augustine in this first chapter because they offer the most basic foundation for thought: that we can achieve certainty on at least this matter of our own existence. I don't think we will find much else that is certain, only beliefs that are more and less probable, more or less justified. But this is not an easy point to swallow; we tend to want our beliefs to be certain. However if certainty, the inability to be mistaken, is a prerequisite for knowledge, it will be hard to find many things that qualify for playing in this league. While it may seem difficult to doubt basic things like the reality of your hands and feet or the tree outside the window, difficult to doubt is not the same thing as impossible to doubt.

The trouble we face is that the beliefs in our heads need to correctly reflect what is outside of our heads, if our beliefs are to be accurate. We are never really in a position to observe both what is inside our minds and what is outside our minds in order to compare them. We cannot get a bird's eye view of the matter where we can see both our beliefs and the world at the same time and see where they match up and where they do not. We are trapped in a sensory shell that we cannot escape in order to verify our thoughts about the external realities. It is thus very hard to be sure that what is inside our minds is an accurate reflection of what is outside of our mind.

But as Descartes and Augustine prove, even if we cannot compare our thoughts with the outside world, we can be assured that there is an "I" who is *trying* to compare them. Using this one certainty as a foundation, we can then step out and try to evaluate what else is at least likely to be true. To do so, we can employ various strategies and devices—the techniques of observation, and logic. The chapters that follow introduce these devices and assess their strengths and weaknesses in pursuing the best possible foundations for our beliefs.

2. THE FIRST DEVICE: OBSERVATION

> Once upon a time it happened that Thor's Hammer fell into the possession of the giant Thrym, who buried it eight fathoms deep under the rocks of Jotunheim. Thor sent Loki to negotiate with Thrym, but could only prevail so far as to get the giant's promise to restore the weapon if [the goddess] Freya would consent to be his bride. . . . Thrym received his veiled bride with due courtesy, but was greatly surprised at seeing her eat for her supper eight salmons and a full grown ox, besides other delicacies, washing the whole down with three tuns of mead. Loki, however, assured him that she had not tasted anything for eight long nights, so great was her desire for her lover, the renowned ruler of Jotunheim. Thrym had at length the curiosity to peep under his bride's veil, but started back in affright and demanded to know why Freya's eyeballs glistened with fire. Loki repeated the same excuse and the giant was satisfied. He ordered the hammer to be brought in and laid upon the maiden's lap. Thereupon Thor threw off his disguise, grasped his redoubted weapon, and slaughtered Thrym and all his followers.—"The Recovery of the Hammer," *Bulfinch's Mythology*

In the search for truth about the world, humans often first reach for our most obvious tool: observation (also referred to as perception). Observation is the use of our senses—sight, sound, smell, taste, and touch—to gather information about the world. Observation may seem like an obvious and reliable strategy in the pursuit of knowledge; after all, our senses seemingly tell us that Bill is taller than Frank or there are more than ten people in a given room. But matters are not quite as straightforward as we might like.

While our senses seem to reveal some of our surroundings to us, it is hard to say exactly how much they reveal. For example, every evening we can watch the sun disappear below the horizon. Our senses tell us a simple story: the sun moves across sky and then sets before nightfall. It took humans a long time to realize that the sun was not rising and setting but rather the Earth was turning.

Over the years instruments to augment our observational powers have been developed: microscopes allow us to observe small things that were previously unobservable, telescopes allow us to observe things that were previously too far away. But while these observational augmentations can help, we still can't be sure we are getting the entire picture. Perhaps even now there are things that are still too small or too far away for us to see, just as germs and some celestial objects once were.

Perception is not only a matter of the sense organs. The sense organs—ears and eyes and all the rest—provide data to the brain, which is the ultimate processor of sensory information. But our senses are the middlemen, and they have severe limitations. We are not in a position where we can see both what are our senses are perceiving and the whole of the external environment and thus determine how much of it our senses are accurately reporting. Without the ability to get outside of our heads and get a direct view of reality, we are left in a state of uncertainty.

Recovery, or the honest use, of sensory evidence is possible if allowances are made in regard to our senses. While we cannot know if our senses are completely accurate, we can seemingly form better and worse conjectures about reality based on sensory data. If our senses could not distinguish freight trains from fields, we might easily picnic on an active rail line and never hear the train. Our senses seemingly do function in regard to our surroundings, the degree and completeness of their efforts, however, is what is hard to determine and gives rise to uncertainty.

It is here that making a conceptual shift in regard to how we think about our sensory evidence becomes important. If we are willing to recognize our senses as flawed and fallible devices, we can start to shift our thinking and speak in terms of probability, likeliness, and unlikeliness rather than in terms of knowledge—which is a very strong word, a powerful concept that implies certainty. We can make a case for more justified and less justified beliefs, despite our flawed sources. The next section introduces some criteria by which these beliefs can be distinguished.

Working Beliefs and Undesirable Beliefs

In the absence of certainty, due in part to the limitations of our sensory perceptions, we must look to form beliefs about reality that are more or less defensible rather than simply true or false. We can think of these as working beliefs and undesirable or bad beliefs. A *working* belief is one that allows or facilitates the effective and efficient achieving of goals or purposes. A bad or undesirable belief is of little assistance in accessing goals and purposes. Working beliefs are understood to be incomplete and unproven, but they are guides that help us on our way.

It is important to remember that working beliefs are tentative. There are two scenarios that should keep us from calling beliefs that are seemingly working as true. First, our working belief could be partly wrong and partly right. For instance, Christopher Columbus believed that the world was round and that therefore he could sail directly to China and the East Indies by heading west from Spain. Given that his beliefs about the matter did not work, they did not get him to China, some of his beliefs about the endeavor were seemingly mistaken. On the other hand, he did not sail off the edge of the world, nor he did sink and he returned to Spain. We are in the same boat in many ways; just because something is working, or does not fail entirely, does not tell us how much we have of the picture.

Second, a working belief could be working for reasons other than we think or be working for apparently no reason at all. A poignant example of this is Ignaz Semmelweis, a nineteenth-century physician who was the first person to suggest that doctors wash their hands before treating patients. Semmelweis instituted hand-washing at the Vienna General Hospital in the 1840s, and the mortality rate of maternity patients plummeted. However, because his colleagues—working in the days before the discovery of germs—did not understand *why* hand-washing worked, they quickly abandoned the process. Semmelweis could come up with no good explanation for why his proposal actually worked, but work it did.

We are thus left in a position of having senses but being uncertain about the extent to which these senses are accurate. How can we make the most of our sense perceptions, despite the uncertainty? One way is to test and experiment with various beliefs and see which bear more fruit. In many ways this is like learning to play a new game; the more you play or experiment, the more you test different strategies or theories, the better one's chances of improving. One never really knows if one is playing the best game possible or that one has not misunderstood some rules, but many times it is still possible to note progress.

Of course, as new beliefs are tried and found to be more effective or more efficient than previous ones, justifications may change. A good belief may later become an unjustified belief, just as an unjustified belief can later become a justified one. Discussing most matters in terms of knowledge is off the table but we do not end in cynicism or full blown skepticism since we can still sort our beliefs by a non-arbitrary system of testing. If something works, if it allows us to scratch an itch, we have a means of testing our beliefs and our observations even though the method is fallible.

Refined Observation

The senses, in a modified form, are thus retained as a means of gathering data about our surroundings. Simple observation, or the idea that our senses completely and accurately inform us of our surroundings, is dropped and is replaced with what might be called a refined theory of observation. We do not know if our senses tell us the whole truth about our surroundings, but by playing and experimenting with our sensory input it is possible to test and thus distinguish better from worse beliefs.

To consider a quick example; on our family farm my father used to separate the bull from the cows for part of the year in an attempt to time reproduction so that calves would arrive in the spring, summer, and fall but not in the cold of winter. My father's beliefs about bovine reproduction could be thought to work—to be accurate—if by using them one was successful in influencing the arrival of the calves. Since work they did, it seems safe to conclude that my father was not mistaken in at least some of his beliefs about this matter.

On the other hand, a belief that by flapping one's arms one can achieve otherwise unassisted flight is easily tested by jumping off a roof while flapping one's arms. This belief does not work, is not justified, if one falls ignobly to the ground. Again, we can ask the question: Does this belief help or fail to assist us in our purposes? The focus on goals is an important clue in how to think. It allows us to connect our beliefs to our surroundings by testing various beliefs, one against another, to see which yields better results, while still acknowledging the limitations of our observations.

To include a final example and at the risk of being over-complete, I would like to consider an example of a good explanation that goes on to become a great explanation. Let's imagine a marriage counselor who interviews a couple, takes notes, and then develops a theory to account for the troubles and successes and thereby develops a recommendation for improving the couples' relationship. The next time they all meet, the counselor explains the theory to the couple, and not only does the theory explain what they had previously told to the marriage counselor but it also explains things they did not mention. What starts as a good theory quickly graduates to a much better theory as it lends further insight into matters not originally considered when the theory was formed. Not only can the explanation do the task required of it, it can also help with previously unidentified tasks, making it a good explanation indeed.

In addition to gathering information it is also necessary to arrange, catalogue and process information and here logic, another study in philosophy, can be of use in keeping our thoughts at least internally consistent.

3. THE SECOND DEVICE: A BIT OF LOGIC

As we saw in the last chapter, observation as a means of gaining knowledge is helpful but limited. Over time and starting with the ancient Greeks, philosophers have been working on a supplement to understanding termed logic. We will focus on deductive logic or the idea that statements need to be consistent to be worthy of serious consideration. Inconsistent thought is bad thought; if two statements contradict each other, at least one of them is seemingly problematic. Consistency, by itself, is not enough to prove something accurate but it is a first test, a condition that must be met in comprehensible thought.

The condition of consistency is one of our best tests of reliable thought. This is why police officers question suspects and witnesses multiple times about the same events. If people can't keep their story reasonably straight, they are probably not remembering it correctly or they are not telling the truth. Consistency is much easier to maintain if you're telling the truth than if you're pretending to recall a story that you've concocted.

Let's quickly turn to some examples where we will only consider short sets of statements to check them set for internal coherence.

Deductive Logic

In a valid or consistent set of statements any conclusions drawn will simply be making explicit what has already been implicitly stated. In logical speak in the following set of statements, the first two statements are premises and the third statement is the conclusion deduced from them:

- All mammals are warm-blooded.
- Horses are mammals.
- Thus, horses are warm-blooded.

If the first two statements (the premises) are accepted, then the conclusion contains no new information, but it does draws information from both premises and thus makes the implicit relations between the two premises explicit in the conclusion. If the conclusion contains new information then it has gone beyond the evidence, a conclusion, properly drawn, is a summation of the information already presented.

Once again a consistent set:

- All candidates for political office play the game of power.
- No one who plays the game of power is an ethical person.
- Thus, no candidates for political office are ethical people.

The first of these three examples, horses, mammals and being warm blooded is consistent and seems to be a mostly accurate description of things. The second is consistent but may or may not be accurate. Perhaps there are some, if not many, ethical people running for office. The job of formal or deductive logic is to test statements for their internal coherence—whether the conclusion is consistent with the premises. It cannot determine whether the premises are accurate. For that we need our first device: observation. Observations about the outside world, while not wholly reliable, can give us information about how many politicians play the game of power and whether power-playing ever coexists with ethical behavior.

Observation is not always needed to test premises. For instance, the statement "All bachelors are unmarried males" is not a matter of observation; it is a matter of definition. In general, however, observation in all its forms—working beliefs, tests, studies, experiments, and so on—are how one establishes the likelihood that a premise reflects the realities of the external world.

Let's sum up this section on deduction with a brain teaser just for fun:

- Nothing is not something for if nothing were something then it would not be nothing.
- Hence nothing is nothing and not something.

The Formal Expression of Logic

Words are bulky. Although we always start thinking of logical scenarios in verbal statements, to test really complex relationships, philosophers have developed a means of translating regular language into almost mathematical symbolic structures. The symbols can take a bit of getting used to, but once you play with this stuff for a while, it really starts to make sense and becomes incredibly useful.

As we've seen, when trying to construct one's beliefs it helps to have a quick test to make sure everything is adding up, at least in terms of consistency. In a sense, logic is the accounting department of the business of forming beliefs. Let's take the following short series of statements:

- If Judy is happy then she will do a good job teaching.
- Judy is happy.
- Therefore she will do a good job teaching.

To translate these logical statements into mathematical form, one replaces the words or phrases with symbols:

J=Judy is happy.
G=She will do a good job teaching.

We'll also use a very specific symbol, the right arrow: $\rightarrow$ this symbol represents the concept "If/Then" and such symbols are central to formal logical expression. The antecedent condition goes before the arrow, and the consequent comes after:

- If Judy is happy, then she will do a good job teaching.
- $J \rightarrow G$

One of the older arguments in philosophy is termed, in technical speak, modus ponens, the "method of putting or affirming," and it can also be expressed like this: $J \rightarrow G$, J, thus G.

The Foundations of Belief

Let's try the same method of expression with a more complicated example, one from philosophy: the importance of ethics or proper conduct. Philosophers debate the source of our moral judgments. Is our morality a purely human affair or are there moral standards that exist outside of us, standards that are universal, established by nature, reason, or God? And does the source of ethical values really matter in terms of the importance of morality?

To help us think through this issue, we first must assign symbols to the important terms or concepts. For this discussion, let's use the following:

- U=Universal moral code based on nature, reason, or God.
- Not U=A moral code not based on nature, reason or God.
- I=Ethics being important

Now we can translate this question into symbolic expressions using the classic If/Then symbol →:

1. U→I: If there is a Universal moral code, then ethics is Important.
2. Not U→I: If there is not a Universal moral code, then ethics is Important.
3. U or Not U: Either there is a Universal moral code or there is not.
4. Thus, I: Ethics is Important.

We can express even more complicated statements by adding other logic symbols:

- ∨ =either/or
- ~=the negative of the statement that follows, so that
- ~ U=Not U

Using these new symbols, we can express the statements above even more succinctly:

1. U→I: If there is a universal moral code, then ethics is important.
2. ~ U→I: If there is not a universal moral code, then ethics is important.
3. U ∨ ~U: There is a universal moral code or there is not.
4. Thus, I: Ethics is important.

A number of additional rules exist for proving the above in a fashion similar to geometrical proofs but this should not be too hard a conclusion for the reader to see. Since it seems that either there is a universal moral code or there is not a universal moral code and since in either case ethics is important, the conclusion that ethics is important follows consistently from the preceding statements. Once again it is important to keep in mind that logic does not tell us if any of the statements under consideration are true or accurate, only whether a set of statements are internally consistent. Each statement then needs to be investigated to determine its degree of accuracy but this is not the job of formal or deductive logic.

Leaving Formal Logic

This is enough logic for the moment, but it should help to give an idea of the role or importance of consistency in helping us develop our working beliefs about the world. There are means of checking our words and thoughts to see if we are following good rules of thinking, if our ideas are comprehensible when they are considered together. Another, and less formal, way of thinking about these matters is to imagine a jigsaw puzzle. To complete the puzzle the separate pieces must be assembled so that they fit together to help make a picture. Beliefs, in a similar fashion, need to fit together to help us see the bigger picture, and when you hammer the wrong piece into place it usually shows.

To continue this metaphor of a jigsaw puzzle, the pictures on the puzzle pieces can be seen to represent the content of our beliefs. The need for the pictures and pieces to fit comfortably together represents the demands of consistency. The puzzle, as it is being completed, represents our attempts to complete a belief structure or an understanding of ourselves and our surroundings. Self-awareness—looking at this puzzle and attempting to determine what one is seeing and what piece might fit with another one—is the believing headquarters that makes the final determinations on these matters.

4. SUMMARY: JUSTIFIED BELIEFS

Plato, an ancient Greek philosopher, when he was discussing belief would distinguish between knowledge and opinion. Plato was seeking knowledge, which he considered to be a timeless, eternal, unchanging truth. Opinion he considered to be almost the opposite of knowledge, as it was unstable, transitory, coming and going with the seasons. For Plato the proper object of philosophical thought, given this distinction, was knowledge.

As the previous chapters have probably made clear, I disagree with Plato as I think there is third category between knowledge and opinion. This is the category of justified (or warranted or non-arbitrary) beliefs. This third category, these justified beliefs, share characteristics of both opinion and knowledge. They are similar to opinion in that they are not thought to be certain, infallible, timeless truths. They are similar to knowledge in that they can be more than thoughts that just come and go; they have some staying power. Justified beliefs, as a balance or mix of Plato's two types of belief, seems to be the modest or more accurate reflection of what we are able to attain with our inquiries and investigations.

For Plato the proper job of the philosopher was to seek out knowledge, timeless truths. But is such a thing really feasible? We've seen that observation is limited by our sense perceptions, and logic is limited by its focus on coherence rather than accuracy. Using both in tandem can give us a more likely picture of reality than we might have otherwise, but leaves us far from certainty. We are forced to settle for the second best option: trying to get our beliefs as accurate as possible but never quite knowing if we are there yet. However, by thinking in terms of justification we prepare ourselves to refine, change, or recalibrate our beliefs and explanations. To think in terms of knowledge is to stagnate and solidify our thoughts and beliefs when they need to remain fluid and open to new evidence.

As the chapters in this part have shown, we do have certain tools at our disposal. First we can be certain of our own existence, our own awareness. Descartes' "I think therefore I am" establishes a clear beginning point for thought. Doubt and uncertainty are thus met with knowledge of my own awareness.

Second, our senses seem to have something to do with ourselves and our surroundings. By putting the evidence of our senses to the test—specifically by testing whether our beliefs about the world work by attaining the goals they are meant to attain—we can shore up our confidence in their input.

Third, if we wish to keep our ideas, thoughts, and beliefs straight we need to be consistent in our use of thought, symbols, and language. Logic allows us to test the internal consistency of our thoughts and beliefs.

In these ways, a crisis of belief becomes mitigated and manageable by a set of workable, non-arbitrary, or justified beliefs that are kept in a somewhat tidy fashion via consistency. These working beliefs are not all random or arbitrary, as they can be tested, one against another, in terms of efficiency and effectiveness. While working beliefs might not provide the certainty we would like, they provide us with ideas about reality that do not seem to overstep due modesty, intellectual honesty, or just plain good sense in thinking about ourselves and our surroundings. (For a longer and fuller discussion of these first four chapters, or Part I, please see my first book, *Some Thoughts on Thinking*.)

Huston Smith provides a more conventional analogy for this process in his chapter on Hinduism in his book *The World's Religions:*

> There is a rider who sits serene and motionless in his chariot. Having delegated responsibility for the journey to his charioteer, he is free to sit back and give full attention to the passing landscape. In this image resides the metaphor of life. The body is the chariot. The road over which it travels are the sense objects. The horses that pull the chariot over the road are the senses them-

selves. The mind that controls the senses when they are disciplined is represented by the reins. The decisional faculty of the mind is the driver, and the master of the chariot, who is in full authority but need never lift a finger, is the ... self.

II

Explanations

5. THE THREE JUDGES

An answer to a crisis of belief just starts with self-awareness which is then supplemented with working beliefs and by tests for internal consistency exemplified by deductive logic. These are the three judges of the validity and soundness of our thoughts. The first in line is the foundation of self-awareness. Self-awareness provides the foundation upon which the rest of our thought is built. It tells us that something (our self, our mind) is definitely there. This self or mind then provides the grounds for attempting to construct other beliefs; it becomes the believing core.

This believing core then is in a position to try out different theories or ideas about how the things we experience function, how they work. As we try out different ideas, we construct working beliefs, which is our best—but always tentative—thoughts about ourselves and reality. Observation, our second judge, lets us test our working beliefs by seeing how effectively and efficiently they are in achieving goals. We possess the ability to continually revise our beliefs through testing and experimenting in terms of achieving goals.

Our third judge in evaluating our working beliefs is consistency, which is expressible through the tools of logic. Logic tests our working beliefs for internal coherence. It is nearly impossible, if not impossible, to imagine an inconsistent set of beliefs that could be considered to be accurate. Inconsistency is the antithesis of working sets of beliefs; it is the antithesis of comprehensible or understandable thought. For example, just as it would be hard to honestly claim one understands what is being said in a language one does not speak, it is difficult to assert you believe something if you have no real idea what the belief means. One may memorize a wise saying or, a phrase, but just learning to repeat sounds is not the same thing as grasping the meaning. Contradictions and inconsistencies cannot be understood by their very nature; while they can be mindlessly repeated they cannot be comprehended.

The Limitations of Observation and Logic

At this point the reader might well be thinking of some objections to the above description of consistency, for instance, the use of counter-intelligence in combat and war. Many times the job of the intelligence office or officer is to spread confusing or inconsistent information to the enemy. If such an effort works, if it yields results, it might seem inconsistency is a viable option in thought.

This, however, is more an example of what might be termed consistent inconsistency. A wise general would not give inconsistent orders to his troops or his intelligence officers; but he might advise his soldiers to confuse the enemy with inconsistent reports. The battle plan is (hopefully) consistent, one might say, but part of the plan is to confuse and confound through apparent inconsistency.

However this example really helps prove the point, when you give someone inconsistent information, it messes with their head. They don't know what to think, what to believe; they cannot sort out a functional or working view of the matter. If sending inconsistent reports were beneficial to the enemy they would not be considered an effective tool of war and conflict.

Another counter-example this commonly raised about the importance of consistency in thought comes from microphysics; according to some descriptions subatomic particles alternate between being one particle and two particles. Imagine, for example, a ball bouncing down a street that for a moment is one ball and then becomes two balls before becoming one ball again and this process repeating indefinitely. However we still need consistency in our thought processes in order to describe our alternating or seemingly inconsistent particles. What would be inconsistent is to say the ball is always one and the ball is always two. If the ball is always one then it cannot always be two and if it is always two it cannot be always one.

The description given of the situation is consistent; it is one, then two, then one, then two, and so on. A universe that pops between two states at minute levels of microphysics is not actually an inconsistent universe. Either micro particles pop or they do not pop, maybe some pop and others do not; but the contradiction is not in the popping. The contradiction is a function of the assertions that "all or some popped" and "none popped" and that "both assertions were accurate descriptions of the behavior of the same micro particles at all points in time." A popping universe is not inconsistent with a popping universe; a popping universe is inconsistent with a non-popping universe.

An additional confusion can also creep in if one fails to consider that descriptions of the micro behavior of objects can differ from the macro descriptions of objects. A single cell is not a person even though all of our organs are composed out of single cells; full knowledge of these cells does not tell us everything about a person. Nonetheless all the cells in combination give rise to something else, a person with a mind, emotions, and beliefs. Describing someone without reference to their DNA and cellular structure is quite different from using solely biochemical terms. Words like kind, generous, and grouchy instead of formulas will be used, but the two descriptions are not incompatible, not inconsistent. One is a microbiological description of the matter and the other a macro or large-scale description that includes mental states, memory, and personality. What is being described is different: the macro description is a description of the whole, the micro a description of the parts.

The same can be said of the history of a country. The full history of a given nation would seemingly have to include a full and complete description of each and every individual that lived in the country, any foreigners that had any influence upon it, every single event that had transpired. It would have to include what each and every one of these individuals did, said, thought, and experienced. If a book on history needed to have such a detailed account of each and every person, assuming this was even possible, it would be so long as to be undesirable for most purposes. Describing history in terms of larger social groups and movements is shorter and less detailed, but the two are not incompatible.

Let's return to the example of the popping particles, micro-particles that pop back and forth between multiple states. These particles when combined in sufficient number, can seemingly create stable macro objects; the basketball that bounces as one and only one down the street. Both descriptions are consistent; it is simply a matter of which end of the telescope one wishes to use to view an object. The optics of the telescope do not change and are not inconsistent, but you might well get a different view of things.

The Ordering of the Three Judges

The three judges all play a vital role in the development of our thought. Issues nonetheless arise when one has three standards of belief justification. What happens if the judges disagree? Is it possible, for instance, for observations to conflict with the demands of consistency? Can an inconsistent set of beliefs work? Can an inconsistent set of beliefs allow for the efficient and effective achievement of goals?

The short answer to these questions is no. Consistency always seems to work. It does not eliminate bad thinking but it does shine a light on particularly bad thought—thought that literally stands in opposition to itself. Any thought that contradicts itself asserts two incompatible descriptions about what to think or how to act. Demands of consistency are derived from demands of how the world really seems to work. The need for consistency, at least in part, is demonstrated by the inability of inconsistent symbol sets to work, to effectively and efficiently achieve goals.

In the end, all three work together. Our awareness sits as the first and final judge in what we accept or believe yet is incapable, by itself, of investigating the external world. Our second judge is observation, which presents us with information for consideration, the building blocks of working beliefs. And the third judge, logic, considers this information and the working beliefs that arise from it in terms of consistency. Together the three judges provide us with a non-arbitrary process of belief justification and seemingly a means of combating doubt.

6. THE JIGSAW SPHERE: A METAPHOR FOR THOUGHT

In the preceding chapters the metaphor of a jigsaw puzzle was used to explain the relationships between consistent beliefs, working beliefs, and self-awareness. I would like to refine this metaphor into what might be termed the jigsaw sphere and add some more players. The sphere, like a jigsaw puzzle, represents the totality of our thoughts and the processes that we use to generate them. But the sphere represents a more developed model than the simple jigsaw puzzle of two dimensions. You can think of the pictures on the puzzle pieces, hard to see with the eye but visible to the mind, as representing the content of our beliefs. And the need for the pieces to fit smoothly is the need for consistency.

The center of the sphere would be self-awareness. This is the core of the sphere, and it connects to all other pieces of the sphere. It is the foundation on which all our other beliefs rest, the base upon which the inner spherical scaffolding is built.

Around this believing core is another layer of beliefs, those related to basic components of our existence, like pain, pleasure, memory, time, space, mathematics, and value judgments. As we move farther from the believing core we start to find more common or ordinary ideas like which sports we like, which political party we prefer, and where the good blueberries are to be found this year. There is no reason to think anyone has exactly the same arrangements of these orderings, or even the same concepts. Most of us seemingly make use of the more basic elements of like memory, ethics, and our experience of time to construct these more specific beliefs. Our ethics may help us to decide with whom we become friends just as our friends can change or beliefs about what is right and wrong. Our experience of pain and our memory may well recommend that we avoid certain foods just as eating new foods can alter one's understanding of pleasurable tastes.

The ordering of these layers might look something like this:

1. The Centerpiece, Headquarters, the Believing Center
2. Memory, Pain, Pleasure
3. Time, Space, Mathematics
4. Ethics, Value Judgments
5. History, Political Views, Etiquette
6. Ordinary or Commonplace Beliefs

The closer to the core, the more basic or general the concept, the more it will play into many other thoughts and ideas. The farther from the core, the more particular the concept or belief and, the less foundational role it plays in other beliefs and concepts. However it does remain connected and potentially influential, if not highly influential, in some cases, on the rest of the belief-net. My experiences of a particular situation can alter my view of values, just as an alteration in my sense of values can alter what I believe about a particular situation.

To see more clearly how the parts of the jigsaw sphere work together, think about your last vacation. You being at the core of the sphere—your self-awareness—remembers the things you did: whether it felt fun or stressful, a painful argument with a friend or a particularly nice time with your spouse. The concepts of time and space in the second layer outside the core are also likely to come into play. You stayed home and worked on the house; you experienced a desert landscape or visited a nice beach. You got lost on a hike, and it felt like you were lost forever. You went on rides with your new girlfriend at an amusement park and the time flew went by very quickly.

Other layers will contribute to your thoughts about the vacation as well: whether you felt poorly served at a restaurant or not, which amusement park had friendly employees. At the end of the day, determinations about whether you made good use of this time off will depend on your concepts of pain and pleasure, happiness, value judgments, what makes for a good or bad day—the sum total of your experiences and thoughts throughout the layers of the jigsaw sphere.

The Jigsaw Sphere in a Crisis of Belief

With the metaphor of the jigsaw sphere in mind, it may be easier to see the effects of a crisis in belief on our thoughts and thought processes. Let's take, for instance, three possible, but not exhaustive, views of time:

1. Time is finite and linear. Time goes from a beginning to an end. The world was created by God and will be brought to an end by God in the final judgment.
2. Time is linear and infinite. There is a beginning but there will not be an end. God set things in motion and in motion they will stay forever; there is no judgment day.
3. Time is infinite and circular. All things that have been will be again and all things that will be have already been. God is the circle.

If you conceive of time as linear, finite, and judgment-oriented (number 1 in this list) but later renounce this concept, many other beliefs are likely to change as you attempt to keep your beliefs consistent. If there is no end of time and there is no judgment day, then maybe there is no morally based afterlife. If there is no morally based afterlife, then social policies, teachings, and laws designed to bring people to this afterlife serve no real purpose. As a result, you might conclude that it is okay to sleep in on Sundays or that you don't need to give money to the preachers on TV or feel guilty about your sexual desires. The list of impact from such a shift in beliefs could be very large indeed.

The Jigsaw Sphere as a Model

The jigsaw sphere is a potent image of the net of beliefs that each of us has. And this net of beliefs is always evolving. These changes often arise from personal experiences: losing your first love can change your view of pleasure and pain. Seeing a tragedy up close may change your ideas about God. But changes in our belief-net can come from outside as well. Studies in psychology can change our views on how memory functions. The study of history can alter our value judgments.

Of course, the jigsaw sphere is not a complete account of mental life. It is merely a way of thinking about how our thoughts play together and create our beliefs. What is missing from it is the inclusion of things like the will, intuition, imagination, personality, providing an account of desire, and so on. A great deal has been packed into the core or headquarters of our self-awareness that needs to be unpacked. But it is a vivid image to help visualize the complexity of our thought processes. It reminds us of our starting point during a crisis of belief: the certainty of our own existence. Around this we can construct a network of belief that, if we are careful, is designed to correct itself over time and keep itself clear of muddled thinking. As Charles Peirce has noted, it is not how often we go wrong that is of interest; it is how often we seem to get things right that is impressive. It may have taken Thomas Edison 10,000 tries to make a light-bulb work but it did not take 100,000, a million, or a billion. If we are constructed of that which surrounds us, then we may not be that different from it and hope for progress in studying ourselves and our surroundings is a real possibility.

7. TWO KINDS OF THINGS: THINKING ABOUT BODY AND MIND

There are a number of questions concerning the existence of body, mind and soul. Before getting started on this, however I would like to give some rough definitions of these terms. Perhaps the simplest of the three to explain is body. The body is essentially matter, something that has weight and takes up space, something that has a physical existence. The toothbrush, the car, micro particles moving in waves all, for our purposes here, are matter or body. Mind and soul are very different from body in that we cannot see them or touch them but we can at the same time experience them in terms of our own awareness, and, indirectly, we can seemingly see them in others. Minds are different from souls in that souls can exist after bodily death and minds dissipate or die upon bodily death; minds share the fate of the body, while souls continue on without a body.

These are commonly accepted definitions, but less accepted is which, if any of these—body, mind, or soul—are real? Which have actual existence? Is mind an illusion, is matter an illusion, do we have a soul? Some parties contend that body or matter is all that exists, that mind and soul do not exist. Others claim that mind or soul is all that exists; we are the product of a dreaming God; matter is but a mirage in the mind. Other schools of thought think mind and body, or soul and body, work together in a fashion not yet understood or understood only by God or other such intelligence(s). These explanations consider matter and mind or matter, mind and soul to be real, to have existence. For these individuals to think only in terms of one and only one type of thing, be it the physical, mental, or spiritual when trying to understand these matters is a mistake.

Each of these possibilities, we might say, is a competing explanation of our reality. They came be summarized like this:

1. Everything that exists is composed of matter and only matter; there is no mind and there is no soul.
2. Everything that exists is composed of mind and only mind; there is no matter and there is no soul.

3. Everything that exists is composed of soul and only soul; there is no matter and there is no mind.
4. Both mind and matter exist; there is no soul.
5. Both soul and matter exist; there is no mind.
6. Both soul and mind exist; there is no matter.
7. All three are real; mind, soul and matter are all things that exist.
8. None of these exist.

The first of the above, the denial of mind and soul seems the hardest of all roads to take. The very act of denying the mind or soul seems to be a mental or spiritual act. Who or what is doing the denying? This is a seemingly clear contradiction, as mere matter would not be aware of itself and could not deny its own existence. Any statement on the very issue of mind/body seems to be a case of matter talking to itself, a strange case of affairs if there is only matter. Matter could bump, rub, induce motion, and change in that fashion, but thinking and talking to itself and to other things?

It should also be kept in mind that, as Descartes and Augustine showed, the most certain belief we have is in our own mental existence. The only thing we know for certain is our own awareness exists; beyond that we have better and worse conjecture but no guarantees. Thus the only thing we can seemingly be certain of is the existence of our own mind, but mind it is, not just matter. This first option that all is matter is thus a bad option, a bad explanation, as it conflicts with and contradicts other experiences for which we have greater evidence; the existence of our own awareness.

The second statement—that everything is mind—while not creating as much trouble as the denial of mind, still seems a bit extreme. Everyday experience seems to yield both animate and inanimate encounters. Some things you look at look back; others don't. We experience ourselves in part as a body; so it's hard to chuck matter overboard and say it is just illusion without further evidence. It just seems to conflict with experience. The piece just does not seem to fit into the puzzle very well.

The third statement—that everything is soul—runs across the same problems as the view that everything is mind. What are these seemingly inanimate things? How are they soul? We might, following some, call inanimate objects "dead soul" or "dead mind," but this seems to welcome matter in the back door after throwing it out the front.

In all of these discussions, we employ the same tools to evaluating these theories in terms of their explanatory value. How well do they work? Does observation, both external and internal (internal observation is also known as introspection), support them? Are they internally consistent or contradictory? The theories that everything is composed of either matter or mind or soul and only matter or mind or soul suffer as explanations. They are seemingly bad explanations as they conflict with or ignore other evidence and experiences.

A Possible Solution: The One That Is Many or the Many That Are Many

We hold that the first three explanations above don't work well to make sense of our experience. We seem to have at least two types of things—material (matter) and nonmaterial (mind and soul)—and yet it is hard to see how they, being so different, could work together. If mind and matter are really different things, how is it that the puppet master, the mind, controls the puppet, the body? If mind is understood to be a real yet an immaterial thing, how could this immaterial thing push and pull the levers of our lungs, hearts, arms, and legs? How could it influence the brain? If we think of mind as a ghost, "a ghost in the machine," something that exists but without any substance, how is this ghost to communicate with the body?

If, on the other hand, we think of mind as a material thing in order to account for the puppet's strings; we run across the same problems as before with purely material accounts of reality. If the mind is an electrical/chemical process in the brain, and this is all it is, then what are these things I experience as thoughts, feelings, and self-awareness? How does an electrical/chemical reaction come to doubt its own existence? How does it come to think at all? We have direct and personal experience of mind; we only have indirect experience of matter through a mind. To have experience is to have a mind; we could not think of matter or the concept matter if we did not have a mind. Mechanical clocks can tell us what time it is, but clocks do know what time they are reporting; they don't think at all.

There are great difficulties in trying to get a final answer to these questions in terms of a theory of reality, nonetheless I do think there are better and worse ways to think about or explain the issues involved and we can draw upon our experience of water to maybe pull us in the right direction. Water is one thing that can take three forms: solid, liquid, or gas. It is one thing that, depending on temperature and pressure, behaves differently. Water is thus an example of one thing that can be many things and even multiple things at the same time. Ice and water can exist and be in contact with each other, influence each other, subsist in the same vessel if the conditions are right. Not an easy blending, however, to keep together if the conditions change too much.

Perhaps we have a basic building block that, like H_2O, can act and behave differently depending upon arrangement and external conditions. Steel can be made to float if it can be shaped to displace more weight in water than it itself weighs, and a handful of plutonium can level a city while a single atom is relatively harmless. It is not only what something is made of, but also how it is formed and shaped that can seemingly make a crucial difference.

Mind and body may be the same thing insofar as they are built from the same ultimate material and yet separate in that they have different characteristics derived from their arrangement. That basic building block would be matter. Matter, in and of itself, is not conscious, though in the correct arrangement it could be. Thus it is potentially conscious. Matter, or the basic building block, as this explanation would have it, is redefined as that which "has weight, takes up space, and is potentially conscious."

In a peculiar or proper arrangement matter realizes a side or aspect of itself that was unrealized before—something potentially present that needs a trigger or a series of triggers to become actual or real. It is like a dormant seed that is placed in soil, watered, and given sunlight. That which was previously inert shows life and in the right conditions can become a tree. To continue the metaphor, imagine this tree does not exist in space, but it does exist in time. We cannot touch, prod, or poke the mind except through the body, but one would not expect a temporal entity, like the mind, to be something observable or detectable in space.

For instance, while the body remains trapped in a specific point in time the mind is free to journey through time, to reflect on the past, to contemplate the future. My mind can journey from one end of the galaxy to the other, far faster than the speed of light. It can travel billions of years in a second when thinking about our cosmic origins and then about lunch. Movement in time and space by a purely temporal entity is quite easy; moving the physical around in time and space, not very easy in comparison.

It is important to note that all bits of matter need not be potentially conscious to account for the regular appearance of mind. Any statistically significant percent of matter could be potentially conscious, but no more, for instance, as this explanation still fits our experiences. What is being postulated is termed, in philosophy and physics, an emergent property. A functioning human brain, by virtue of its functioning, is aware; it generates a shadowy entity that exists in time but not in space. There are thus two types of things, bodies and minds—or, to say it another way, brains and a purely temporal awareness that is nonetheless seemingly tied to that brain.

The main difference between this theory and the first three discussed is that it does not attempt to explain away, to dismiss, either matter or mind. This theory does not try to say that mind or matter is ultimately an illusion. Neither are illusions, in my view of a good explanation, of the issue at hand. Mind and matter are both real even if they are products of something more basic that is shared by both.

One can skate upon ice even though it is ultimately the same thing as water and skating upon ice is not an illusion because ice is ultimately the same thing as water or steam. Neither mind nor matter cease to exist just because they are composed of something that is not identical with them. My mind is not an illusion just because it needs electrical/chemical processes to function. Matter does not cease to exist just because one needs a mind to perceive it.

How this process works, how mind and brain exist together and work upon each other, still remains a good mystery. I don't know of any good explanations of this process of communication outside of the fact that it really seems to happen. We see them both act independently every day: I can decide to go to the movies (mind over body) and if I cut myself while cooking it hurts (body over mind).

Another possibility in this category of both mind and matter being real is that of multiple ultimate building blocks instead of just one ultimate building block. Water is a molecule built out of atoms, which are built out of even smaller and smaller particles. If this trend continues to the final analysis, we may find two or more fundamental things, none of which is mind or matter as we understand the terms but nonetheless are responsible, in their respective arrangements, for the world we live in and experience. If a single building block is "the one that is many," then multiple building blocks would be "the many that are many" that still, when in a particular or proper arrangement, realize mental experience.

Either way, there is still mind and matter. There is interaction, communication between the two. How this communication transpires is still a mystery, however. If we are still uncovering newer and even smaller particles, there would seem to be good reason for this being a mystery as we, at best, have only a partial understanding of the issues at hand. Both of these possibilities seem to be better explanations as they do not deny our experiences of either mind or matter. Nonetheless they both leave something to be desired as an explanation since the method of communication between mind and brain is left unexplained. The suggestion is that the communication is similar to the interaction of ice and water in the same vessel; ultimately they are close enough to pass information back and forth but a metaphor without a literal exposition still lacks as an explanation.

It does, however, offer some explanation of the power of the mind. The body is trapped in time, moving in one direction; the mind, being free of physical constraints, can journey through time. We can remember the past and make plans for the future, all because the mind or soul is free from bodily constraints to move freely in time. A soul might easily experience things just as the mind experiences things with the difference being that a soul can continue to exist after the death of the body. Instead of mental death when the body expires we would have a continuation of personality and/or memories in a form of disembodied life.

Substantive evidence of disembodied mental life is the critical component that is lacking for giving good reason for putting souls into the mix of things. We have evidence of embodied mental existence; I can experience this myself. We do not have, however, reliable evidence of minds that exist outside of bodies. I have never experienced this myself and nearly all, if not all, the reports of it are suspect for one or many reasons. It is possible though to believe without or beyond the evidence and thus come to the conclusion that souls are real. In the fifth and final section of the book I will discuss belief that is based neither on observation nor reasoning. Concepts like faith, hope, and trust are explicable and perhaps best understood in their application, and I will leave this issue until then.

The Two Things and the Limitations of Language

A final consideration on this topic has to do with explanation 8, the final option: that none of these three, body, mind, soul, exist or are real. It may be true that none of these three exist—but only because our language may not be up to the task of accurately describing true reality. There may be little reason to think that English (or any human language) in the early twenty-first century is ready to provide the conceptual, linguistic, and structural resources necessary for full comprehension. For instance English uses a noun/verb structure; persons, places, or things are all taken to be nouns. However, people, places, and most things change—maybe not quickly but they do when looked at over long or very long periods of time. The only things that do not seem to change, that seem to endure over time, are things like subatomic particles. The use of nouns, on any but the smallest of scales, may thus be a misconception of reality when applied to anything but the most fundamental and basic constructs of existence. And a language that misapplies itself so thoroughly is hampered in its efforts of description of the totality.

With this in mind one might argue that mind/body/soul are all inadequate ideas and need to be abandoned in light of the problems one has with language. It is hard, however, to say that nothing exists, as our mental existence precludes this possibility. Nothing may be as we suppose, but this does not mean there is nothing and not something as there needs to be that which supposes in order to have a mistaken supposition. As always, our self-awareness is the surest foundation that we have.

Explanations and Their Explanatory Value

The recommended solution—the fourth explanation discussed earlier—has the virtue of not denying either mind or matter. Thus it is the best choice among competing explanations. When you have competing explanations, you must compare each with experiences to see if they fit, if they are consistent with other beliefs, and if they work efficiently and effectively in getting at things. Yet even after such a comparison, you may end up with an unsettled issue. While one of the options may appear better than the others, none is not without some trouble. Inquiry is like this at many times; one can label some explanations as bad but still not be in a position to settle a matter conclusively. Explanations, when they rely upon working beliefs, suffer the same malady of being fallible and incomplete.

8. ON THE FREEDOM OF THE WILL

> The future appears as a realm of contingency and freedom, not, like the past, as a closed record of unchangeable necessity.—F. M. Cornford, "Before and After Socrates"

Out one of the great questions of philosophy hovers over all our discussions; that of free will versus determinism. Are we really thinking freely about these beliefs, or are we limited from the start by deterministic factors that dictate how we think about them?

As with most great questions, an extensive variety of answers has been suggested and to sort through these would take another book or two. However, it is possible to distinguish between those philosophers who allow that we have influence over our decisions and those who do not allow that we have influence over our decisions. Advocates—to one degree or another—of the former might be termed to be in the free will camp, and those that argue in favor of the latter are in the determinist camp. What it means to say a will is free I will leave until for a moment as these two camps or schools of thought are enough to get the discussion started.

The past appears to be closed, final, static, and dead; the future appears open, full of possibilities, dynamic, in motion. If we are looking backward, a deterministic explanation or description seems to make more sense. When one looks to the future determinism seems misconceived as an explanation or a description as choice seems to be in operation, at least from time to time. This provides some initial evidence for the existence of free will—if we had no experience of a free will, I doubt there would even be a question to dispute.

It is also hard to explain the how, why, or to what purpose a deterministic universe would include a vocabulary that pertains to decision and choices. Terms dealing with violation and deliberation would have no application as there would be no decisions or choices to be found in a deterministic reality. Words like ethics, morals, justice, right, and wrong would have no purpose and would have no reason to exist or to be employed. Given that the existence of single term that referenced a free decision or a free choice would be inexpiable in a deterministic reality, we have an abundance of justification for considering matters in terms of postulating a free will. I directly experience the guiding of my own thoughts; in this I seem to have an awareness of being aware and I seemingly directly experience free will. I also have an awareness of concepts like justice, ethics, right and wrong, regret, and an old-fashioned sense of honor. None of this would be possible in a universe with brains but no minds, and the experience of directing one's own thoughts would not seemingly be a possible experience in a purely material and determined universe.

It is more difficult, I think, to give an adequate account of what free will is because what an undetermined choice is not so easy to spell out. If a free will is understood in terms of a random process, this does no more justice to our experiences in terms of accuracy of an explanation than determinism does. If my choices are just random, then I have no control over the process and things like virtues, ethics, and attempts to live a better life are all pointless in terms of affecting any change. Given that I can correctly criticize and praise myself—that saying to myself, "Jon that was a stupid thing to say, I should have done this, etc."—is not a pointless forum, then more than a random process has to be in play.

Taking a hint from Cornford, as quoted at the beginning of the chapter, making distinctions among past, present, and future might prove useful. While material or physical existence may exist concurrently with our minds, matter can only be observed in the past. The very nature of external observation requires that the observed event or events have already transpired, even if only a micro-moment before. One cannot literally observe the present or the future unless one is doing it in one's mind or imagination. Our minds seemingly straddle both the past (memories) and the present (conscious thought) and are able to think about the future (planning ahead).

We might begin understanding a free will thusly, as the ability to draw upon the past or our memories, in the present, for the purposes of hopefully changing the future. John S. Mill will say something similar in his *A System of Logic*, in the chapter on Liberty and Necessity:

> And, indeed, if we examine closely, we shall find that this feeling, of our being able to modify our own character *if we wish*, is itself the feeling of moral freedom which we are conscious of. A person feels morally free who feels that his habits or his temptations are not his masters, but he theirs: who even in yielding to them knows that he could resist; that were he desirous of altogether throwing them off, there would not be required for that purpose a stronger desire than he knows himself to be capable of feeling. It is of course necessary, to render our consciousness of freedom complete, that we should have succeeded in making our character all we have hitherto attempted to make it; for if we have wished and not attained, we have, to that extent, not power over our own character—we are not free. Or at least, we must feel that our wish, if not strong enough to alter our character, is strong enough to conquer our character when the two are brought into conflict in any particular case of conduct. And hence it is said with truth, that none but a person of confirmed virtue is completely free.

9. SUMMARY: ALLIGATORS AND LADDERS

One of the goals of inquiry is the explanation of experience, and in this chapter I want to dig deeper into what is intended by this phrase. A good explanation of experience, in this system of thought, is given in terms of attempting to match working and consistent beliefs with what we experience. A good explanation is thus one that fits with our experiences, can help us understand them or work with them, and is consistent with other things thought to be accurate.

A bad explanation, on the other hand, is one that does not fit very well with our experiences, does little work, and has little support from other beliefs. A terrible explanation makes little or no sense of our experiences, is likely to be counterproductive, and conflicts with other beliefs that have greater support. Great explanations will fit our experiences, achieve the desired results, are supported by other beliefs, give further insight into other matters, and tend not to be falsified by new experiences. And to complete a list of five, a terrific explanation is one that fits our experiences, significantly exceeds one's expectations in terms of results, fills in other missing pieces of the puzzle, and stands the test of time quite well with little needing to be added or subtracted.

Our goal, of course, is to move from inferior explanations to better explanations. One example of this shift is a story that my father used to delight in telling. When I was a child, and before I had learned much of anything about bodies of water, I had determined, for some reason or another, that there were alligators living in our nearby pond. I came up with a plan to use a ladder "to get at the alligators" in the pond. It is not clear what I intended to do once I "got them," but my thought process went something like this:

1. There is a pond to which I have surface access but not easy underwater access.
2. There are alligators underwater in the pond which I want to "get at."
3. When Dad does not have easy access to something he uses a ladder; and thus . . .
4. If I want to "get at" the alligators in the pond I will need a ladder to climb under the water.

I explained something like this to my father when he found me trying to take a ladder from the garage, and he has explained it to many others since.

I had reached what seemed to be a good conclusion given points 1, 2, and 3 but it was nonetheless mistaken. Getting beneath the water is not like trying to get to something on the roof. My explanation of how to get underwater, in light of my experience to date on how to get to hard-to-reach places, was seemingly justified yet also inaccurate.

An explanation that has always worked in the past can suddenly hit a brick wall and utterly fail when put to use in an untested situation. What has been a good explanation can very quickly become a bad one, as in my ladder thesis. Additionally it is possible for a good explanation that has become a bad one to become a good one once again; it just depends on the evidence gathered over time and one's other beliefs. It is theoretically possible for an explanation to run the spectrum of terrible to terrific once or many times during its span of use.

While it does not happen to everyone, some will experience something like this in regard to a belief in a personal God, believing and not believing at different points in their lives. Explanations, when they rely on working beliefs, must also be treated like working beliefs. We can have a seemingly good explanation that matches our experiences to date, but as our experiences can be incomplete or atypical in some fashion, the explanation may not be as good as it appears. We need to approach our explanations like our beliefs and keep in mind that they are fallible.

Very good and very old questions in philosophy center around human conduct, what is proper, correct, right, good and what is improper, incorrect, wrong or evil. With our three judges understood as a process of belief formation and justification, for the purposes of providing explanations about ourselves and our surroundings, we can begin attempting to match our experiences with explanations of ethics. Given that we are dealing with a flawed and fallible process this needs to be kept in mind when discussing standards for human behavior. Some of the greatest injustices in history have seemingly been enabled by thinking of ethics in terms of being certain.

III

The Search for Ethics

10. ETHICAL REALISM: THE SEARCH FOR ETHICAL FACTS

> In every system of morality, which I have hitherto met with, I have always remark'd, that the author proceeds for some time in the ordinary ways of reasoning, and establishes the being of a God, or makes observations concerning human affairs; when all of a sudden I am surpriz'd to find, that instead of the usual copulations of propositions, *is*, and *is not*, I meet with no proposition that is not connected with an *ought*, or an *ought not*. This change is imperceptible; but is however, of the last consequence. For as this *ought*, or *ought not*, expresses some new relation or affirmation, 'tis necessary that it shou'd be observ'd and explain'd; and at the same time that a reason should be given; for what seems altogether inconceivable, how this new relation can be a deduction from others, which are entirely different from it.—David Hume, *A Treatise of Human Nature*

In the previous two parts of this book, we have examined the tools that we have at our disposal to develop working beliefs about the world. In this part, we focus in on one particular set of beliefs: those regarding proper human behavior, often known as *ethics*.

Despite the tools we can use to construct working beliefs, sometimes evidence for a particular belief set is simply not available. When faced with this situation, there are two general ways of proceeding. One option is to stay put, philosophically speaking, and not commit one's thought any farther until one has good reason for do so. Another option is to come at the matter differently, to attempt a re-conception of the issue or issues involved. This means taking a peek at what might lie ahead as one waits for further information before making a decision. This process of taking a peek, even though one is not certain this path will be the one eventually selected, is what I define as hypothetical philosophy. In this chapter we will use some hypothetical philosophy to investigate ethics.

With the above in mind I want to make a general distinction in ethics and then follow the less traveled road on this distinction. While I inclined to the side of the distinction I am about to out-line, I do not think there is enough intellectual grounds on which to conclusively settle the matter. I will nonetheless present, in the following, some of my concerns about what I will term 'realist ethics' but I want to make clear that I don't think these concerns decisive.

Does an ethic or set of principles have some kind of universal, objective basis? Or is ethics a function of human decisions with no foundation in enduring natural or divine principles? We considered these options briefly when we discussed formal logic and considered a short proof of the importance of ethics, and now we will give those names: ethical realism and ethical non-realism.

Let's look first at ethical realism. This is the belief that ethical standards or judgments have an existence independent of human thinking. Ethical realists believe that when somebody does something wrong, that person has broken some ultimate code applicable to everyone. They believe that rules of conduct exist that are eternal and universal and that these rules are not just created by humans who are responding to temporary and changeable circumstances.

Ethical non-realism is the belief that ethics is dependent upon human or self-reflective thought and that we cannot check our view of it against some objective source. Ethical non-realists believe that codes of conduct are not derived from some ultimate and final law of God or nature but instead are determined in choice or judgment. Some non-realists believe that there are no codes of conduct that are ever applicable; these are ethical non-realists of a nihilist stripe. Nihilism is different from other forms of ethical non-realism in that it rejects all values. Ethical non-realism can admit values, just not in the same way that a realist program of ethics determines values.

The primary difference between realists and non-realists is in how they understand the reality of value judgments. If you think value judgments are discovered and not invented, you are more of a realist. If you think they are invented you are a non-realist. Science tends to discover things; art tends to invent them. Planets, atoms, and microorganisms are discovered; money, the Mona Lisa, and Sherlock Holmes are invented. An ethical realist will tend to see ethics as more of a science, as an existing fact to be discovered; a non-realist will see ethics more as an art that is crafted in self-reflective thought.

Ethical non-realism is different from ethical relativism, the view that all ethical judgments are equal regardless of their content. An ethical relativist sees all ethical judgments as equal; an ethical non-realist is not committed to this understanding. While ethics is invented and not discovered, this does not preclude some inventions from being better than others. Terming something more an art than a science does not preclude judgments about the quality of the art. Just as some painting are of higher quality than others, so some codes of conduct, even when crafted by humans, will be of higher quality than others.

Establishing Ethical Facts: The Basis of Realist Ethics

The basis of ethical realism is establishing ethical facts. Consider the following situation:

1. Person S (person starving) does not have enough food to survive and will soon perish.
2. Person W (person wasting) lives very near to person S and has so much food that it is rotting and going to waste.

Statements 1 and 2 are facts, but they are not *ethical facts*. They do not tell us whether the person with surplus food should assist the person who is starving. To arriveat an ethical fact, we need to go further:

1. Person S does not have enough food to survive and will soon perish.
2. Person W lives very near to person S and has so much food that it is rotting and going to waste.
3. Persons with excess food that will rot and waste should, if possible or in near proximity, give or sell this food to another in need.

Statement 3 here is the supposed ethical fact. At this point, it is just an assertion. How do we determine that this fact is true or real, that those with excess food actually *should* donate or sell it to those without? Observation and reasoning, working beliefs and consistency, can establish many things, including the existence of poverty and abundance, but how do they establish ethical facts? We can demonstrate that two men have been hanged or crucified by finding their bodies. It is not so easy to demonstrate whether they were hanged or crucified justly or unjustly. Science does not seem to be of much use in such questions. Which instrument or experiment should we use to determine the justly hanged or unjustly imprisoned: a telescope, microscope or a psychological study? It is hard to see how any ethical statement is not a value judgment.

Ethics appears to be a decision made by an individual and not a matter of exterior fact. There may be people with better and worse ethical judgments but this does not mean these people are working from ethical facts. The trouble with establishing ethical facts is that they, like our minds, do not seem to be directly observable by others. Observations and reasoning might help us in determining how a person died but it does not seem these devices can speak to the justice of the matter.

Using Public Opinion to Establish Ethical Facts

One way to establish ethical rules is to determine what popular opinion is on various behaviors. In this method, we would observe, test, and interview many people. Pollsters do this on a regular basis: They ask a representative sample of a given society whether they approve or disapprove of different kinds of behavior. Other researchers go beyond this kind of self-reporting and do long interviews and detailed observation to determine what people's attitudes are toward various behaviors. Once we determine what people's attitudes and behaviors are, we can average them and recommend these averages as ethical behavior. For example, if we find that 95 percent of drivers speed but only 1 percent drive while intoxicated, one can assume that, at least in the society being polled, speeding may well be considered acceptable behavior but driving while intoxicated is not.

There are problems with this polling method, however. If we polled the citizens of Athens about the time when Socrates was forced to drink poison, we might find approval of his execution. The same might be said of Jesus's execution a few centuries later. Yet both executions would now be seen as unjust. The list of behaviors that were once acceptable but now condemned—slavery, feudalism, segregation, disenfranchisement of women, homosexuality—is long. We see that the polling method is unreliable because public opinion can be swayed by such things as the pressures of war, the belief in traditions, self-interest, ignorance, temporary stresses and passions.

The passage of time itself introduces ethical innovations, new ways of understanding behavior and its effect on others. If we reject ethical innovation, we might as well base our behavior on that of chimps and apes, which presumably have experienced less ethical innovation than modern humans. And a kind of reverse engineering regarding ethics can show the limitations of the polling approach as well: if ethical behavior is defined as whatever is the norm, then deviations from that norm must be unethical. If this understanding of ethics leads us to condemn as such figures as Socrates and Jesus, then perhaps this understanding is insufficient.

Taking the average and labeling it as good is much like labeling average grades as excellent and labeling both the excellent and not-so-good students as the bad ones. It would mean that the runner, who finishes not first, not last, but in the middle, wins the gold medal and is "the fastest." It would mean that if only a few people have the courage of their convictions then they are actually morally diseased. The most common behavior is not necessarily the best behavior.

Even so, a good deal can be learned by ethical polls, interviews, and the study of primates. Large amounts of data can often help in making much better determinations about any subject matter. Gathering and collecting data on ethical judgments can thus be a vital part of the investigative process in ethics, but this method does not seem well-suited for passing final judgment. Contemporary communal appeals can take one only so far in ethical thought. The community and one's contemporaries are not always the best decision makers. Even our own behavior can be consistent, but consistently selfish. We need something more.

Using Religion to Establish Ethical Facts

Because human judgments about ethics are so unreliable, so often altered over time and geography, we often look outside ourselves for guidance. The oldest and most common source appealed to for ethical fact is religion or revelation. It is the common view that God(s), through books, prophets, or personal visits, has provided humankind with codes of conduct. The word of the divine is our bond; what he/she/it/they have spoken we should do; the supernatural has shown us the path of how to live correctly.

The trouble with this approach is that unless you have had personal experience with a divine spokesperson you are left in the position of taking another's word on the matter. This is the method of *faith,* which is really the antithesis of philosophical thought. Even if you turn to priests or philosophers for guidance, you should get a chance to examine their ideas for yourself and evaluate how they reached their conclusions. It is one thing to accept directions to the supermarket from a friend or stranger but another thing to craft one's most important beliefs in the same manner. Trust and faith are how we describe forming beliefs on matters beyond the evidence and I will leave this discussion until later. Given the limitations of opinion and religion or revelation, it's possible that the search for ethical facts is in vain. Perhaps another approach is warranted. In the next chapter, we look at the non-realist approach, which instead of searching for ethical facts looks at *ethical judgments*.

11. NON-REALIST ETHICS: THE SEARCH FOR ETHICAL JUDGMENT

> Ethics, too, are nothing but reverence for life. This is what gives me the fundamental principle of morality, namely, that good consists in maintaining, promoting, and enhancing life, and that destroying, injuring, and limiting life are evil.—Albert Schweitzer, *Civilization and Ethics*

Because establishing ethical facts is so difficult, perhaps non-realist ethics is a more fruitful direction to try. At some level—realist or non-realist—ethics is about making a choice, deciding to try and behave properly or correctly. But while realists like Plato will want ethical facts or universal, timeless principles on which to establish their ethical views, non-realists will be more open to establishing the principles of ethics in judgments, which rely on human decision making rather than some super-human standard.

Ethical non-realism allows us to develop ethics in the same way we develop etiquette. Etiquette is the rule set that governs small and relatively insignificant categories of conduct: talking on the phone, conducting a job interview, responding to gifts, meeting strangers. They are rules that smooth our interactions with others and help create a pleasant society. You may think that etiquette is just a matter of taste, and sometimes this is true. But there are many matters of etiquette that seem to work, that do seem to help in achieving the goal of social harmony. We don't purposely spit on other people when we are being introduced; or seriously harm others for fun and expect them to be our friends, nor do we mislead others when we want their trust.

Etiquette may vary from culture to culture, but we can still evaluate which sets of etiquette work better and remove bad choices from the mix. Etiquette practices that were developed before the germ theory of disease may not be as good as those that take it into account. Bowing our heads, for instance, when meeting and greeting instead of shaking hands might make for better health and thus be recommendable on these grounds. Both show respect but one does not include the physical contact that can transmit some diseases. Rules of etiquette may not be universal, but they are not all equal, and we can sort between them and find the better ones, over time.

Ethics works in the same way as etiquette, simply on a larger, more important scale. Ethics is intended for the public good and social harmony—to enhance life, as Albert Schweitzer noted. And although ethics may vary from culture to culture, some ethical systems may be judged better than others. For example, ethical theories developed before the idea of universal human rights may not be as good as those that take them into account. While it may not be an ethical fact that humans have rights, it might be better to act as if that were true, or to make the determination, the decision, to treat others with respect, as though they truly had these rights.

If we want both others and ourselves to have reasonable success in meeting, greeting, and cooperating with others, then something like etiquette and ethics is needed. The careful reader will note, however, that the above statement is a conditional one: if we want to successfully cooperate with others then we need etiquette and ethics. If one does not want to cooperate successfully with others then one may not think etiquette and ethics a good or necessary idea. The conquering warlord who thinks he has no use for the local population may not think the ethical treatment of these people to be important. I would think him wrong in this judgment, but I do not think the invisible heavens will shudder even if he kills all the locals he meets. His is a choice, even if a bad one to those who think ethics is important.

Ethics as a Choice or Judgment

Ethical non-realists see ethics as being a choice, a choice between deciding to value life or not to value life. It is a judgment. To value life and respect yourself and others is what it means to be ethical. Ethical facts do not enter into it the way they do with ethical non-realism. There is no outside set of rules to which you, the ethical person, are adhering. The only fact is the fact of your own choice. To say it another way, if you fail to respect or value other people, you may not be at odds with some universal code but you will be likely to find yourself at odds with the many and probably yourself as well. To not respect life is to find that you are at odds with what it is to be a human; you are in conflict with your own humanity—that part of yourself that Aristotle called the "social animal." The matter is similar to choosing or not choosing to study mathematics; while there is nothing objectively wrong about being mathematically illiterate it is still true that you are mathematically illiterate. Similarly if one has decided not to value life or any life beyond one's own this choice is not objectively wrong, but in this system it will qualify one as being unethical.

When discussing working beliefs, we saw that one way to judge beliefs is to evaluate how well they work at achieving their own goals—whether the goal be explaining why objects fall to earth or creating a society with a low level of violence. If the 'goal' of ethics is to promote life, then it is possible to compare various ethical systems and find that some are better or worse at valuing life and creating social harmony. If humanity is indeed a social species the substance and structure of standards of conduct will need to take this into account. A rule prohibiting all speech, for instance, would probably not work in most settings. If the three great basic drives in humanity are food, sex, and sleep, social systems that deny or hamper these drives would not function as well as others if our goal is to have happy, prosperous, and content members of a society.

Ethics as a Life-Creating Choice

So how do we judge which conception of ethics is best at achieving the goals of enhancing life and promoting social harmony? For realists, there is really only one choice: to follow the universal ethic or not to follow this ethic. In this sense ethics is fixed, determined, and eternal, even if it is currently not a well-lit path. It is the life that must be walked if you are to be ethical. Ethics is understood as a form of will-full enslavement, the happy serf of the invisible heavens. The rules of conduct are set; if the social world deviates from those rules, then the social world should be altered to reflect these universal rules.

For non-realists, however, things are not as straightforward. Non-realists create their own rules, fashioning an ethic that fits different personalities, circumstances, talents, weaknesses, cultures, and so on. Ethics is not seen as some eternally fixed standard but as an unfinished book that asks readers to write their own sentences, paragraphs or chapters if they find they have something to add. Ethics is more like Wikipedia than the Encyclopedia Britannica.

Let's take some considerations on punishment as an example. Justice or valuing life demands the enforcement of standards of conduct, and this enforcement usually entails punishing those found guilty of violating these standards. Various judicial methods are possible but some seemingly work better than others, at least in certain contexts. According to some accounts, swift, sure, and moderate punishment is the most effective in deterring future crime. If there is a very good chance of getting caught and if punishment is administered in close temporal connection with the crime and is reasonable in terms of the crime, law-breaking declines. Low conviction rates and considerable time lapses between action and reaction, even if combined with harsh punishments, are not as effective in deterring crime.

Circumstances, however, can create an environment where certainty of capture and short lapses of time between action and reaction are not possible. Thus one is left only with harsh punishments if one is to have any significant impact on conduct. The American Old West comes to mind as perhaps an example of such an environment. It might take years to bring someone to justice for cattle-rustling, but the person might be hanged for it. While this approach may not be ideal, it may be the best rule for the circumstances. Ethical non-realism recognizes this reality and deals with such situations and finds a way of promoting life, growing like a plant towards the light, even if it must creep through cracks in the side-walk. Realist ethics are more like words written on stone, more dead than living, and the ethical realist appears as the surrogate Moses.

The Best of Both Worlds

Despite the limitations of realist ethics, this school of thought can still have a role to play. One of the interesting things about non-realist or life-creating ethics is that it is still possible to draw upon the realist ethical literature when constructing one's point of view. Formerly realist ideas can be converted to non-realist ideas by understanding them to be ethical judgments and not ethical facts, by reading them from a life-creating point of view. Thus just as one could read what was written as fantasy as if it were reality, one can also read what was written as reality as if it were fantasy. While I don't usually recommend viewing fantasy as reality, I can and do recommend, in many cases, viewing what is labeled truth as fiction. It should be noted, however, that many realists are very likely to object to this process of reading their truths as fiction. No true believer wants to be told that his belief system "has some good points."

For a non-realist, developing good working beliefs about ethics can be like developing a food menu, drawing upon the best that different cultural cuisines have to offer. With this in mind, the next chapters draw from the thought of perhaps the three most influential thinkers on ethics in Western philosophy. The first is Aristotle, a student of Plato, who wrote in the fourth century before Christ and was called simply "the philosopher" by Saint Thomas Aquinas. The second is Immanuel Kant, a late-eighteenth-century Prussian philosopher and author of some of the more difficult reads in philosophy. The last is John Stuart Mill, a nineteenth-century British philosopher, the son of the philosopher James Mill and probably the most famous advocate of utilitarianism.

12. CONVERTING A LITTLE BIT OF ARISTOTLE

Ethics, of course, is not just one thing. The diversity of behaviors encompassed by ethics is large and wide. One way to categorize them is by the range of people affected by them. From this point of view, we can draw some general distinctions between what might be called personal ethics, character ethics, and social ethics.

Personal, Character, and Social Ethics

A purely personal ethic deals only with the self. Studying, exercise, or meditation, if done solely to benefit one's self, would be considered a purely personal ethic. Part of valuing life is taking the time to be concerned with the functionality and talents of your body, brain, and mind. But a personal ethic is very limited in its reach. Character ethics covers how we go about ordinary life and interactions with others, such as dating, shopping, working, and living in the same house with family or roommates. Social ethics contains elements of political theory and deals more with how we think society should be set up and run. Labor laws, judicial systems, and national policies are examples of social ethical thought. These three types of ethics can overlap. A purely personal ethic can overlap with character ethics when we speak of the work ethic of a person, just as a social ethic can inform one's character ethics when one starts a recycling plan in the office or work-place. What is intended in thus more of a continuum ranging from conduct focused solely on the self to conduct focused on the behavior of all. Valuing life includes taking oneself and others into consideration when determining how to behave.

For various reasons, one of which might be the comparatively small size of their society or city-states, some of the ancient Greeks developed, what I consider to be, a very good system of personal and character ethics. It is possible to expand their conceptions to contemporary social or business ethics but that is a discussion for another time. In the ethical system being outlined here, personal ethics and character ethics will involve the concept of human excellence or virtues. Good people are those who possess virtues, and to be a good person at the level of character and personal ethics is to cultivate these human excellences.

Examples of virtues are courage or bravery, temperance, generosity, wit, and honesty. However, the basic concept behind each virtue remains the same. A virtue is a human excellence, or the better path, in a given sphere of human conduct. Wit, for instance, is the virtue or best path governing the sphere of socializing, courage is the virtue that deals with fear and generosity the virtue dealing with money or resources. According to this theory we are good people to the degree we have developed these virtues and bad people insofar as we have not developed these virtues or have developed their opposites, vices.

For Aristotle, in his *Nichomachean Ethics*, virtues are defined as a middle ground between two extremes of behavior characterized by deficiency and excess—a moderate approach to behavior that is also known as 'the golden mean'. For example, if we look at the behavior of eating, it is possible to eat too much or too little. What is a good diet may differ from person to person, but keeping our bodies fit is part of what Aristotle called temperance. It's not always easy to hit the mark, perhaps, but to be temperate is seemingly good advice, a means of keeping a check on what can be self-destructive or even socially-odorous appetites. Gluttony, addiction(s) and obesity are not good, life-promoting habits, just as self-starvation makes little sense unless there is a greater goal in play.

Examples of Virtues

The idea of the golden mean works well for thinking about most types of behavior. Some behaviors, like infidelity or murder, are put out of bounds and do not admit of a mean or a balance between two extremes. Here we will look at three examples of virtues that are a means between two extremes: generosity, wit, and truthfulness.

Generosity is the virtue connected with the use of money and resources. It is the middle ground between the extremes of profligacy and miserliness. A good person is not one who gives everything or nearly everything they have to others. A wise person, a generous person, does not give to silly or ineffectual purposes or give so much as to cause themselves, their friends, and their families' hardships. One could donate your entire salary and all your assets to college scholarships, for instance, but then you would become a great burden on others, if you are to keep body and mind together. To never assist others in life, on the other hand, when you have some extra means or resources, seems a bit wrong-headed. The good or generous person walks the middle ground between these two extremes and gives proportionally to his or her means and other obligations, and they give in the right circumstances. The miser is as out of touch with this virtue as the spendthrift.

Wit is the virtue covering the sphere of socializing or social entertainment. To always make a joke, no matter the context or who it hurts or embarrasses, is to go too far and become a buffoon or an ass. To never attempt a joke, to never engage in light, clever, or jovial conversation is to be a bore or a stiff. The recommended or best path is to be aware of one's setting, to whom one is speaking, and to keep this in mind when trying to have some fun in conversation. The best path is to have fun in conversation and social events; this is not possible if you are offending people or if you don't try a joke or two.

Truthfulness is the virtue connected with describing oneself to others. The boaster, the individual who makes too much of his or her accomplishments, is one extreme. While the self-deprecator, the person who makes too little of himself or herself and downplays what he or she has done, is the other extreme. For Aristotle the excellence is to have an accurate assessment of yourself and to put this forward when you are the subject of conversation.

Truthfulness, for Aristotle, only relates to how a person talks about him- or herself. But we can consider other types of truthfulness as well in terms of another virtue not discussed by Aristotle, *honesty*. Honesty is the best path regarding conversation or communication on any topic, outside of social entertainment, or the arena of conduct described under wit. As long as it is made clear that a joke is a joke, one need not worry about stretching the truth. A good roasting, for instance, many times depends upon exaggerating faults or character traits.

Extrapolating Aristotle's definition of virtue as adherence to a golden mean, the honest person is one who strives for accuracy in communication, does not fail to include relevant concerns, but does not feel the need to say everything on his or her mind. Too much honesty is saying everything you think or feel. Too little honesty is saying things you don't really think to be accurate, telling only partial truths or failing to include pertinent information to the audience.

Identifying Virtue: The Case of Honesty

Identifying virtues and vices would seem to be a straightforward matter. If a statement is intentionally inaccurate, it is a lie and the teller is dishonest. But when we dig deeper, we see that this is not always the case. The complexities of identifying virtue can be explored through the case study of one virtue, honesty.

One can be dishonest in many ways. For example, by changing tone, word order, grammar, emphasis, body language, and so on, it is possible to literally say one thing and communicate the opposite. In cases like this the spirit or intent of what is being presented is different from what is stated. Sarcasm, for instance, reads very differently in a literal sense than with the sarcastic tone included. If you are to be honest, then both the spirit and the letter of that which is communicated needs to correspond with what you really think.

Dishonesty can also occur through lying by omission. Describing a reward to be won without mentioning the dangers can be even more deceptive than outright falsehoods. Partial truths tend to be more convincing, more believable, for the very reason that they are partly true. If one is omitting what the listener is likely to consider relevant information and the reason for this omission is to deceive the listener, this is not honest behavior.

Beneficial deceptions are another good question about honesty and one can really take three roads on this matter and still seemingly be an honest person. A military training drill, for example, might well require that the trainees be unaware that it is a drill. The first road on the matter is to say that deception is never justified, no lie, no breaking with honesty is ever allowed. The second road on the matter is to say that deception is never justified unless the possibility of deception is disclosed in advance. Thus one cannot deceive potential trainees without first informing them that part of their training may involve some false drills, etc. They agree to be deceived and this agreement justifies the deception and preserves the virtue of honesty.

These two approaches, never lying or never lying without first securing agreement over the potential deception leads to certain types of problems, the 'inquiring murderer' for instance. If a wild-eyed and dangerous-looking person holding a long knife asks where he might find someone you are familiar with, you might be inclined to hold your tongue. However, if you knew the lunatic was getting close (he is in the right neighborhood, his intended victim works right across the street, etc.), holding one's tongue may not be enough. Misdirecting the 'inquiring murderer' and then informing the relevant individual(s) and authorities, while being dishonest, would not seem to make you a bad person.

The third approach, that of, allowing deception in extraordinary circumstances thus seems the more sensible path when combined with second approach as well. It is here that it is useful to pull again from Aristotle and note that the virtues need to be something practiced over time. They need to be habits, deeply ingrained patterns of behavior, to count as virtues. One cannot be generous once and thereby become a generous person; one cannot make a single joke in one's whole life and be witty. In the same fashion being an honest person is about communicating, in both spirit and letter, what you think to be an accurate description of matters over time. The rare case of deceiving in extraordinary and compelling circumstances would not seemingly stand against a record of honesty when evaluating the characteristics of a person.

The white lie, especially if it is expected, is a case similar to agreeing to be deceived. Not every moment is one of serious conversation about the state of the world, the universe, ethics or the totality of our experience of existence. Being gracious or even, a tad flattering in social environments is thus more a question of what type of social manners one prefers, courtly or otherwise, than it is a question of honesty. I tend to prefer less flattery and more directness in these questions of etiquette, but honesty here is understood, like before, as probably not saying everything on your mind and not being deceptive.

There are other issues involved in a conception of honesty as well. For instance, children may ask questions about mature or adult subjects that you don't wish to discuss. Or an individual may try to pry secrets or information from you that you don't wish to divulge. Even here, though, there are ways of responding that don't violate honesty. "This matter really doesn't concern you" is a good response. Changing the subject works as well if you are dealing with polite people who have pushed too far. One can be honest while not allowing others to take too much of an advantage of the situation. Nothing in being honest requires one to answer any given query or even pay it heed.

Other questions can be asked of this virtue; can one be deceptive in times of war, in spying and counter-spying, under-cover police work, etc.? However I think we have spent enough time on this particular virtue and need to return to the larger discussion. The general concept is that if you are intentionally deceiving others or you have no selector switch on what you communicate then you have missed the virtue of honesty. With the above in hand I would like to suggest something like this as a quick example of a character ethic and a personal ethic. The above small set of virtues, if a person is very good at sticking to them over time, would seemingly make one a better person than an individual who did not develop them. This list could easily be expanded and just as easily it could vary from person to person or culture to culture. Other systems of virtue-based ethics could be selected, there is no need to use Aristotle, for instance, but the overall process remains the same; a choice is made to follow an ethic that values life beyond just the self.

13. CONVERTING A LITTLE BIT OF KANT

I intend to spare the reader a good deal of hair pulling by not going too deeply into Kant's ethical system described in his *Foundations of the Metaphysics of Morals*. Instead I will focus more on his conclusions. There are a number of reasons for this time-saving move. 1) Kant is complex on this matter. 2) Good treatments of Kant's ethical system already exist in layman's terms, (see James Rachels' *The Elements of Moral Philosophy* 2nd or later editions). 3) I don't think the discussion of it would add much to the point I am working toward at this juncture. The following has been termed "The Second Form of the Categorical Imperative" or "The Formula of the End in Itself." However, we can shorten this to 'Kant's Second Imperative' for our purposes here.

Kant's Second Imperative is this: "Act in such a way that you always treat humanity, whether in your own person or in the person of any other, never simply as a means but as an end also."

This simple statement is actually quite profound when it is explained in a bit of detail. A means is a method of getting to something; treating someone as a means indicates treating them like an instrument, a thing to be used to get to something else. An end, on the other hand, is a purpose that guides actions and decisions, a goal that is desirable in and of itself and not simply as a steppingstone to some other goal. Thus to treat someone as an end and never only as a means requires that another person's interests, wants, needs are taken into consideration when dealing with them. It means that the person's well-being is something desirable in itself. It requires never just using the person for one's own purposes.

With a little bit of work this simple phrase can be cashed out into one, two or all three of the distinctions mentioned earlier; a purely personal ethic, a character ethic, and a social ethic. In terms of a purely personal ethic, an ethic aimed only at ourselves, Kant's formula instructs us that we have a responsibility to take care of and improve ourselves. If we value ourselves as we should, we should develop our talents rather than, say, sit around watching TV all day. We will take care of our health and exercise our gifts. To do nothing with one's self and one's abilities is to fail to respect one's self. Of course, a personal ethic alone is not sufficient to be considered virtuous. An ethic only applying to your person is not a terribly robust form of valuing life as it simply fails to value more than one life.

In terms of a character ethic—an ethic for home, work, and friends—this idea of treating others as ends and never as a means seems to be an equally good guide. When one treats others as ends, one treats their needs and wants as part of the equation; they, just like you, need to be considered in making decisions. Stealing, lying, raping, murdering, short-changing, and committing fraud are all examples of things that can happen when treat others as means. Charity, honest conversation, and displays of kindness are examples of what can happen when you treat people as ends.

Finally, Kant's Second Imperative seems to be a very good foundation for a social ethic. Social ethics encompasses ideas about human rights and the areas of human behavior that are embedded in institutions, rather than just individuals. For example, businesses should not use people's labor and fail to pay them for it. Armies should not unnecessarily harm civilians or anyone for that matter if one can win the day without fighting. Governments should not unnecessarily eavesdrop on citizens or seize their assets. Individuals, in Kant's ethical system, should be treated with respect, and their interests should not be dismissed or unduly minimized—including by institutions like businesses and government. One way to help ensure a good social ethic is to encode human rights into law. Laws, policies and governments can be established, administrated, and enforced in light of human rights understood on this basis.

Kant intended his system to be a complete ethic, but it is possible to use it as any of these three, or any combination of the three, when choosing to value life. Like Kant, I think it best to use it in all three areas of ethical thought. Unlike Kant, however, I do not think that this ethical system by itself is the best available ethic or method for valuing life.

14. CONVERTING A LITTLE BIT OF MILL

The foundation of Mill's moral philosophy is less difficult than Kant's and he stated his general ethical principle with brevity:

"The creed which accepts as the foundation of morals 'utility' or the 'greatest happiness principle' holds that actions are right in proportion as they tend to promote happiness; wrong as they tend to promote the reverse of happiness."

Mill's "Greatest Happiness"

There are two important components of Mill's formulation. The first is the idea of happiness. Mill uses the term happiness in his definition but, given some of the contemporary connotations of this term, we might be better off using the term *contentment.* Actions are right or good insofar as they aim to promote the contentment of all involved, including one's self. Actions are wrong insofar as they don't promote the contentment of all or the opposite of contentment. Contentment, in this sense, is not meant to differ from Mill's conception of happiness: "not a life of rapture, but moments of such, made up of a few and transitory pains, many and various pleasures, with a decided predominance of the active over the passive, and having as a foundation of the whole not to expect more than life is capable of bestowing." Contentment is used here simply to get away from the meanings of happiness that focus too much on rapture or states of extreme pleasure.

Mill also distinguishes between higher and lower pleasures, better and worse pleasures; in sum, "it is better to be Socrates dissatisfied than a pig satisfied." For Mill the better pleasures are the ones preferred by competent judges, those who have experienced both pleasures in question. A life of bodily pleasure, while it might seem to be the best life, is really not all that much fun when compared with life that holds higher quality pleasures. Inferior pleasures are only of the moment. They are mindless entertainments and cannot fully satisfy. Higher quality pleasures have the potential for application and usage beyond the now or the moment.

Attempting to determine the best ways to promote contentment is where Mill's theory starts to get a bit complex. Many types of actions, as Mill notes, can be ruled out pretty quickly by reference to history, be it personal or from the history of the species. Showing too much trust and loyalty to humans is not wise just as never trusting is probably a mistake; blood feuds are far worse than having a system of impartial justice. The truly best paths are not always immediately clear but better ones maybe discernible with time and effort.

The second important component of Mill's formulation is the idea of the "greatest" happiness. For Mill, actions are right or ethical to the degree that they produce the greatest amount of happiness for all involved and wrong if they fail to promote the greatest happiness for all involved. The need to consider the "all involved" is an often over looked aspect of this theory for first-timers, and many people run off thinking Mill is saying, "do what makes yourself and only yourself the happiest," when he is in fact saying something very different. When acting, we need to consider the impact on all that will be affected by our actions. A life of thievery might make one person happier but it is likely to make the other people less happy; and all people need to be considered when deciding on what to do.

In sum, Mill outlines a system of ethics that focuses on what will bring the greatest amount of happiness/contentment to the most people. This system has implications for personal, character, and social ethics. In the area of social ethics, for instance, we may need to have prisons or forms of punishment but we should try to devise methods of behavioral correction that bring about the best possible results. If humans respond most effectively to swift, sure, and moderate punishment, then we should devise swift, sure, and moderate systems of punishment when it is possible to do so. If, on the other hand, slow, uncertain, but harsh punishments bring about more happiness/contentment than other judicial systems we should use slow, uncertain, and harsh punishments.

Secondary Ethical Principles

Mill, in his book *Utilitarianism,* also uses the concept of subordinate and secondary moral principles to supplement his main or primary principle of ethics. For Mill, when it comes to judging ethical matters, the greatest happiness or least pain is the final or supreme adjudicator. However, lesser ideals or standards can be added and are operative over our judgments until they come into conflict with this supreme principle or other standards. In cases of conflicting standards the greatest utility is used to settle the dispute. It's possible to show the relationship of these standards graphically:

Final Standard: The greatest happiness, the least amount of pain.
Sub-Standard A: Do not kill.
Sub-Standard B: Do not lie.
Sub-Standard C: Do not steal.
Sub-Standard D: Protect, feed, and defend yourself, your friends, and your family.

It should not be a difficult to see how sub-standard D, our need to protect, feed and defend might conflict with standards A, B and C. If someone was trying to harm your family one might think it best to deal with the threat rather harshly if the police, for whatever reason, are not of much use. If your family is starving, telling a lie or stealing some food might seem much better than the hunger and eventual death.

It is here where the first standard is so useful, when lesser ideals come into conflict, when our moral judgments are in conflict; a method of resolving these conflicts is available. One should not lie, but to avoid death by starvation, lying seems the lesser of the two evils and thus perhaps permissible in such circumstances in Mill's thought. Murdering someone, however, to acquire a winter's supply of food for one's starving family, if one could have acquired it by petty theft, would be very wrong. It would be prohibited by the final standard as it causes more harm than just stealing. In these cases Mill has provided us with a test, a final arbitrator, to resolve the matter. We will return to this theme of ethical conflict resolution in the next chapter where we will tie these three ethical theories together.

15. PUTTING ALL THREE TOGETHER

While I have presented these short selections of Aristotle, Kant, and Mill as independent ethical systems, because they are independent ethical systems, it is possible to put them all together into a unified system of ethics that draws upon the strengths of each. For myself, such a unified system would start with Kant's Second Imperative—to treat others and ourselves always as an end and never as means only—as the baseline or starting point. Respecting other people as ends, respecting their rights, immediately throws all sorts of nasty behavior out the window. Murder, slavery, deception, false promises, stealing, and attempts to disregard the legitimate interests others are not allowed. It is a solid bulwark against many of the most serious ethical violations and a reminder to be considerate and take care of oneself.

After establishing this baseline, cashing out some of what it means to treat ourselves and others as ends allows Aristotle and his conception of virtue easily to come into play. To develop yourself as an end, in part, is to develop more than a few virtues in addition to your non-ethical talents. A good person is thus one who respects the rights of others, respects him- or herself, and develops temperance, generosity, truthfulness, wit, honesty, and so on, in addition to their other talents or abilities (singing, competing in sports, etc.).

The final layer to this system of thought is using Mill to solve ethical conflicts that can arise from these former commitments and/or when the first two fail to speak adequately to a moral question. It can be hard to fully respect an enemy's life in war, and it is times like this that Mill becomes very useful. While it is the case in this unified system that we should treat others as if they have human rights, it is also true that, due to circumstances beyond our control, respecting everyone's rights equally is not always possible. In war or some other extreme situations, defending the lives or rights of some may involve taking the lives of others. When parts of an ethical system come into conflict, it is essential to have an overall judge to which one can make appeals—and the principle of "greatest happiness" and the concomitant hierarchy of standards can serve just this function.

Treating another as an end, for instance, requires a bit of charity from time to time, as does the virtue of generosity. You might find, however, that you have many in need but insufficient surplus in your pockets to meet all the needs. At these times the principle of utility would tell us to give resources where it is likely to do the most good.

This may seem a bit like common sense but some cases are more complicated than others. For example, part of respecting the rights of others is to respect the fruits of their labors. If a person or family purchases some land, works the land, and improves the land, it is hard not to see this property as the person's property and something that cannot be taken away. Cities and growing populations, however, can push up against the boundaries of farms and ranches. If some of the properties of these landowners are needed to build more efficient means of transport, housing, or commerce, one gets into a conflict of interests and rights.

In this case the landowners' rights to the products of their labor are in conflict with the need for others to move efficiently between home, town, and work. Because of this, even though it does violence to the landowners, it seems permissible to compensate the landowners and use what is needed in terms of the greater community. However, to make up for the harm to the landowner, the level of compensation for their land needs to be considerable—twenty times the market value perhaps—as the violence that is done is considerable. Such over-valued compensation would also help ensure that governments only take such extreme measures when absolutely necessary. The rights of many are in play and not all can be fully respected, but the harms can still be minimized as much as possible. This is perhaps the best overall outcome as it takes the rights of both very seriously and attempts to preserve the farmers' right to liberty, which seemingly needs to include the rights to the product of their labor.

To summarize the matter in a form of short statements we get the following ethical system or means of valuing life:

1. Act in accordance with Kant's principle of treating others and yourself never as a means but always as an end.
2. Develop Aristotle's virtues, such as temperance, generosity, truthfulness, wit, and honesty.
3. Use Mill's principle of greatest contentment as the final ethical judge in cases of conflict within or between the first or second principles, or in ethical cases where they are silent.

This is one system of many that can be proposed; ethical non-realism can come in many forms. Choosing to value life is a principle that all life-creating ethics have in common, but it may be the only element they have in common. Outside of requiring a rather robust concept of valuing life, life-creating ethics leave a good deal of room for individual innovation. It does seem likely that, as time passes, general agreement between many, if not most, can be reached on at least what are the glaringly ineffective means of valuing life. While the human body and mind does not come with an owner's manual, this does not mean we cannot try to write one. Ethics is not a place where all answers are equal. Neither is it a realm where speaking in terms of knowledge, truth and falsehood, shed much light. But over time, better manuals can be sorted from less effective manuals.

Other Tools for Crafting an Ethic

This synthesis of realist and non-realist ethics—encompassing the thoughts of Aristotle, Kant, and Mill—is just one possible life-creating ethical system. It can also be seen as an attempted synthesis of Plato's timeless, eternal truths and what he terms transitory opinion as ethical non-realism has aspects of both just as justified beliefs have aspects of both. This combined system focuses more on being a certain type of person—one who respects the rights of others, values them as ends and practices a number of virtues. Ethical reasoning, in full gear, enters the mix when there is conflict within or between these previous commitments, at which point reasoning aims at preserving as much of these previous commitments as possible.

Another possible approach is valuing life by concentrating on ethical or moral reasoning more than focusing on being a certain kind of person. In this alternate approach ethics is a function of thinking matters through in terms of various ethical standards and then deciding in terms of these ethical standards. Employing concepts like fairness or impartiality, kindness, honesty, and respect become the coin in which ethics is trafficked. To behave ethically, to value life, is to employ these and other ethical concepts when one makes determinations about matters of conduct. To behave poorly is not to use these and other concepts in matters of conduct. (A good introduction to this approach is Stephen Cohen's *The Nature of Moral Reasoning*.)

Another way to think about ethics begins with a distinction that is often made in ethics between positive and negative morality. Negative morality covers prohibitions: do not steal, do not lie, do not murder. Positive reality covers our duties or obligations to help others. It is not enough that we should not harm other people without just cause; we should also render assistance in some cases. Negative morality is usually much easier to get some general agreement on, as murder is pretty universally condemned as is kidnapping, rape, assault, and so on. Positive morality is much harder to get agreement on and the reasons for this are many and varied but the difficulty remains. Thomas Aquinas suggested that negative morality should be the subject of law while positive morality should come from example, usually from civic leaders. Not a bad idea if one's civic leaders are up to the task.

Thus one method of solving these concerns over positive morality is to embracing a system of negative morality while leaving positive morality purely to each individual. Such thoughts can be found in libertarian political views and are not a bad way of thinking about behavior, although not free of difficulties. Still it provides another example of a possible ethical system assuming that one's conception of positive morality is robust enough.

Another approach is the contract theory of morals or contract ethics. In some of these contract models ethics, we acknowledge that we have made a theoretical contract with each other for the purpose of safety and survival. That is, we have given up political independence for some form of government and thereby avoid a short, miserable life holed in a cave half-starved and mostly sleep deprived. In this system, we have an obligation to uphold our responsibilities as members of the contract that we have agreed upon for mutual survival and well-being. What types of rules that the contract encompasses varies depending on circumstances and the author doing the recommending; but as such systems tend to be founded on self-interest, they have a solid basis in human psychology.

Contract ethics ultimately sees ethics as a matter of pure prudence, and this introduces some difficulties. If a person decides to be ethical only for the sake of prudence or staying out of trouble, is this individual truly ethical? If a person behaves only because it is in their best interests, might they not then misbehave if misbehavior becomes clearly prudent? Since stability of ethical character marks a good person over time, it is hard to admit the purely prudent into the circle of morality.

Nonetheless ethics has some potential personal benefits in addition to the societal benefits of valuing life. Plato discussed the potential perks of ethical behavior in his anecdote of the lion, the beast, and the man:

> "Imagine, to begin with, the figure of a multifarious and many-headed beast, girt round with heads of animals, tame and wild, which it can grow out of itself and transform itself at will."
> "That would tax the skill of a sculptor; but luckily the stuff of imagination is easier to mold than wax."
> "Now add two other forms, a lion and a man. The many-headed beast is to be the largest by far, and the lion next to it in size. Then join them in such a way that the three somehow grow together into one. Lastly, mold the outside into the likeness of one of them, the man, so that to eyes which cannot see inside the outward sheath, the whole may look like a single creature, a human being."
> "Very well, what then?"
> "We can now reply to anyone who says that for this human creature, wrongdoing pays and there is nothing to be gained by doing right. This simply means, we shall tell him, that it pays to feed up and strengthen the composite beast and all that belongs to the lion, and to starve the man till he is so enfeebled that the other two can drag him wither they will and he cannot bring them together to live in peace, but must leave them to bite and struggle and devour each other. On the other hand, to declare that justice pays is to assert that all our words and actions should tend towards giving the man within us complete mastery over the whole human creature, and letting him take the many-headed creature under his care and tame its wildness, like the gardener who trains his cherished plants while he checks the growth of weeds. He should enlist the lion as his ally, and, caring for all alike, should foster their growth by first reconciling them to one another and to himself."

For Plato, in his work *The Republic*, our minds are a combination of three drives or psychological forces: the appetites, spirit, and reason. In the above passage Plato represents our appetites by the many-headed beast, our spirit or will by the lion, and our reason as the man among the two beasts. If we can achieve the proper balance between these drives, it becomes possible to live in a state of mental harmony rather than one of internal conflict.

Indeed if these drives are in a state of ongoing conflict, difficulties with others and yourself may not be far away. If your appetites are out of control, another form of control, natural or human, is likely to come and speak with you. If your spirit or emotions go too far, you may continuously find yourself in unnecessarily heated disagreements, not speaking with one's family for years or hell-bent on a self-destructive search for revenge.

Mental health is thus a byproduct of ethical behavior. When one's mind is divided and this conflict is serious enough, one is very likely to have an unpleasant mental life. If the divisions go too far, highly abnormal behavior can result. For instance, if one loves and hates something, one might well find oneself in orbit around it, never getting too close, never too far and never moving on.

Insofar as we are social animals, ethics can make human association much easier. Insofar as this socializing is part of our needs, wants, and mental health, being ethical seems to scratch more than just one itch. Ethics helps pave the way to better human relationships and it can spare one the mental anguish of the warring mind. I would not be surprised to find that ethical thought also benefits the physical body, in a fashion similar to how depression can negatively affect one's physical health, but nothing herein depends upon this being true.

This insight is of particular importance to the problems of contract ethics. Although contract ethics relies on the idea of prudence and avoiding personal harm, Plato suggests that ethics creates a unity between what is good for the world and what is good for us.

16. SUMMARY: A GUIDE BOOK

In the preceding pages I have argued that not all goals are ethically equal and I had defined working beliefs as those that allow for and facilitate the achievement of goals. I now would like to combine these concepts and discuss how to determine better or worse goals. This is a question I promised to address at the end of my first book and should lend some substance to my phrase 'leaving an issue to another time' as the second book exists mostly to answer this question.

We started this discussion of ethics by distinguishing between realist and non-realist approaches to ethics. The realist approach sees ethics as something universal and external to humanity. The task of the realist ethicist is to determine *ethical facts*—principles that are true. Non-realists, however, abandon the search for ethical facts in favor of ethical judgments. They admit room for disagreement on ethical behavior but assert that there are ethical and unethical judgments of a conditional and better-and-worse kind. While ethical judgments in ethical realism appear more as true or false, right or wrong, in ethical non-realism, ethical judgments appear as equal, better or worse, wise or foolish. There are two other ethical approaches as well. One is nihilism, which by its own definition is dismissed from ethical consideration as it denies the legitimacy of any and all ethics. Nihilism is a way of looking at or thinking about ethics but it is not an ethic in itself; it is a point of view on ethics. The second is relativism, the view that all ethical judgments are equal. This may also be rejected since some types of behaviors are just not very good at valuing life. Hitting people in the head with big heavy sticks will not do much to promote life and will most likely have the opposite effect. If we value life, not all patterns of behavior are equal.

Nonetheless when you make a choice to value life your subsequent decisions and actions can become restricted, which is the point of an ethic. You cannot just do anything you like to other people if you value their life. Poisoning them, pushing them off cliffs, etc., out of the behavioral question; looking after their physical and emotional needs is most likely part of the equation. If you choose to respect and value life then there are things that can and cannot be done in terms of this valuing and respecting. In ethics it is if, if, if . . . not is, is, is . . .

Ethical thought doesn't exist in a vacuum but is informed by the circumstances in which it finds itself, and when we choose to value life we seemingly choose to value the guide-book for that life as well. It is hard to justly claim that we care about another person if we have no idea about the individual in question, his or her needs and wants, who and what he or she is, the actual person. In a similar fashion it is hard to justly claim we value humanity if we have no idea about the human creature itself. Good intentions without first doing our homework can result in wasted effort at best and counterproductive results at worst. Acting without study or thinking is a form of ethical recklessness.

Thus if you choose to be ethical, if you choose to pursue goals that are ethical, you need to choose goals that are consistent with the well-being of the creatures who will be affected. It does little good to try and care for a fish if you remove it from water for even a short period of time; the poor thing will just not live that long. Likewise one can behave in certain ways that cause people discomfort, severe discomfort, or even death. In these cases, it looks like you are not doing a very good job of valuing these lives unless some form of ethically purposeful punishment is being applied. Even then, a particular type of punishment may be counterproductive and actually hurt society, if, as Socrates suggests, those who misbehave need education and not punishment.

Part of the guide book of humanity seemingly can and has been already written in both our own personal experiences to the collected experiences and history of the species. Using our experiences as a guide, it is fairly easy to see what works in enhancing life, what brings more smiles than tears. Acting ethically means taking things like human rights and human contentment seriously. It means taking the time to form justified or non-arbitrary beliefs about ourselves and the surrounding environment and a means of forming better and worse judgments about what is and what is not proper conduct. As life-creators in an open society we are left with very little certainty, but we are not completely in the dark and have perhaps found a bit of a resolution to a crisis of belief. While a citadel of certainty would be a better ending to the story, such a reality is likely to be found only in fairy-tales. It is perhaps better to be flexible and prepared to alter our beliefs in accordance with the realization that we are many times mistaken about what we think and believe.

IV

Political Economic Belief

17. MORAL MINIMUMS AND DEEP VALUES

There was a time, not so long ago in geological terms, when people's environment and external circumstances determined nearly all of their economic choices. The vast majority of people lived a rural existence where they mixed labor with animals and the earth via basic technologies to provide for their wants and needs. In these times of limited technology, there were simply no real options when it came to supply and demand, production and distribution. Most everyone was needed to work the land, to provide the basics of life, and that was that, so to speak. Political thought was thus mostly devoid of economic thought. Most discussions in politics focused on the proper ways to honor the god(s), distribution of power and determining who would do the fighting and who to fight. The questions that engaged Plato, Aristotle, St. Thomas Aquinas, and their contemporaries were questions of political power and how it was to be wisely distributed.

This situation was nearly static for quite some time, until the rise of what we call modernity around the fifteenth century. New technologies and forms of social organization came into existence and with them new options in the production, transportation, and distribution of goods, services and power became possible. What was once termed political theory began to consider matters of economic importance as well, and thus political economics was born.

A good measure of how advanced, or dependent, a society is on technology is the percent of its population it needs to commit to feed, clothe, and shelter itself—to provide the basics. As fewer and fewer people are required to produce and distribute these basics more time can be devoted to other ends or goals. When a society requires only a fraction of its population to produce the necessities, to what other ends should that society devote its excess resources of time, money, labor, and so on? After all, the possibilities are almost endless: such a society now has the ability to pursue any number of projects: medical research, free college education, civic constructions, building a powerful military, funding the arts or producing fashionable clothing.

To begin any political organization, however, one needs some rules of the road on how to pursue whatever goals are selected. One needs a system of social ethics, a system of social rules. Even a pure despot needs to inform others of their new rule, what they do or do not want done and how this or that will get done. One suggestion for some cooperative rules has been termed "the moral minimums," or the deeper value commitments needed for any society to survive over time.

These minimal value commitments are three in number:

1. Prohibitions against murder and assault. It is nearly impossible to get people to meet and greet in public if they have no good reason to think they will not get killed or hurt. I would not meet my classes, for instance, if I thought there a real chance on any given day that one or all of my students might try to hurt me. I doubt my students would come to class if they believed they were likely to get seriously harmed for their efforts. Given that we need to meet and greet to conduct the necessary business of society, efforts to curtail murder and assault are necessary. This does not mean that no one ever gets hurt or killed, but this risk needs to be quite low.
2. Procreation and education of the young. Humans grow old, retire, and perish, and thus new members of society are needed. And if they are to fill the shoes of their elders, they need to be trained. Thus, if a society wants to continue over time it needs to provide for the procreation and the education of its newest members. This does not mean everyone needs to procreate or that everyone will be educated, just that if a society does not reproduce it will die out over time. The survival mechanisms and strategies for advanced forms of cooperation must be transmitted to the young if the society is not to slowly dissolve into something more primal.
3. A commitment to truth-telling. Communication is a social necessity as cooperative efforts are difficult to pull off without communication. Be it in writing, over the phone, body language, sign language, emoticons, or something other form, language and the use of it is a big part of social life. Now imagine a society in which every communication was always a deception. Why would anyone ever bother talking, writ-

ing, or signaling in any fashion? An expectation and tradition of truth-telling is a prerequisite for effective communication. For a society to flourish, it isn't necessary for everyone to tell the truth all the time, but it necessary that deception is the exception, not the rule. If deception becomes the rule instead of the exception discourse would seemingly come to an end and so any of the benefits to be realized by communication.

Many thinkers have devised lists similar to the above. John Locke, for example, outlines his basic value commitments in *The Second Treatise of Government*, which include (1) the rights to life and freedom from assault, (2) liberty, and (3) estate or property as a basis for creating an ethical political association. Thus if we take something like these moral minimums we can then add other ends or social goals depending on what type of society is desired. Capitalism, for instance, seems to require a commitment to private property and liberty in one fashion or another. This does not mean capitalism is good or proper form of political economic organization; it may or not be depending on which values one wants to realize. But *if* a society wishes to pursue capitalism, private property and liberty are some of the moral and legal commitments seemingly required.

Libertarian conceptions of economic justice, for instance, are different from egalitarian conceptions. The former distributes rewards and penalties based more on success and failure. The latter distributes rewards much more evenly, though perhaps without matching the productive output of libertarian systems. Many modern societies favor a mix of these two in an attempt to gain the productive power of libertarian systems with the social safety nets of egalitarian system. Providing a viable social safety net, providing for the procreation and education of the young, dealing with those who flaunt prohibitions against assault and the taking of life, all require a reliable economic engine.

In any case, while it is usually more confusing to have options, overall it seems better to have more options than less, so that is good news. Fortunately recorded history provides us some good examples of what to avoid and what to pursue. The next chapter looks at some lessons that can be we can seemingly glean from history.

18. CLOSED SOCIETIES AND HIERARCHIES

In any belief system, one of the most important tests of its soundness is whether it works to achieve the goal it was intended to achieve. Like ethics, political economics has the goal of creating a social good. Therefore we can look at the various forms of human organization throughout different places and times to see if they have worked to produce that good. Social experiments in political economics have the downside of having far too many variables for one to be certain as to why or how this idea or that may have failed. But a lack of certainty does not preclude thinking in terms of warrant or justification.

History, for instance, seemingly provides plenty of warning about the dangers of closed societies. Closed societies are societies that attempt to maintain their traditions at the expense of innovation. This structure can have many attractive qualities but circumstances beyond their control can pose insurmountable troubles for them. The bubonic plague of the fourteenth century was just such a circumstance. Its' devastating toll—a third of Europe's population—forced changes to the prevailing feudal systems of Europe, and those changes cumulated in the rise of the rise of the nation-state, democracy, and the open society. Basic innovations in sanitation, science and medicine, for instance, might well have reduced the death toll. Had the disease been better understood people could have been advised not to gather in the churches to seek divine forgiveness for imagined sins as they spread the plague to even more. Of course open societies will face similar threats, but they seemingly have a better chance of finding solutions because innovation is part of their culture. An open society, as it embraces innovation over tradition, is more prepared for changes and can learn to anticipate some of them as well if the society is well educated. Of course, open societies may face different kinds of danger—the danger of Dr. Frankenstein and his monster, Icarus and his wings, the consequences of incautious experimentation—so perhaps a balance of innovation and tradition is to be preferred. But it would seem that at least aspects of the innovative nature of the open society are desirable in one form or another if we are going to be even somewhat prepared make needed changes brought on by circumstances beyond effective social control.

History can also teach us about the need for hierarchies and the need for limits on hierarchies. Hierarchies imply power differentials, in which those few at the top have a much greater say in decision making than the many at the bottom. It is hard not see hierarchies as perhaps one of the greatest unnamed human evils, given the infliction of unnecessary harm that it usually involves. However some form hierarchy may well be necessary, it is just one of the realities one must face in terms of human organization. To get things done, at some point deliberation usually needs to be replaced with action, and in cases of disagreement this means a method of deciding is seemingly required. Small societies may use methods that are more egalitarian, like the Quakers' and talking until they all agree but with large organizations this might not be possible. This is also true in systems of economic organization that employ private property, in which the will of the property owner often takes precedence over the will of the wider community when the owner's property is concerned.

The need for hierarchies seems to have permeated modern political systems as well. Although the ancient Athenians embraced a system of direct democracy, in which the entire citizenry voted on each proposal, modern democracies rely on hierarchies. A president gives commands to his executive branch, the Supreme Court interprets laws for the entire nation, and countless small administrative decisions are imposed on residents daily, ranging from the cost to use the municipal golf course to, in some communities, which colors homeowners are allowed to paint their houses. Hierarchical control is always dangerous because one person (or a small group) has authority over the autonomy or even lives of others. To command another is an awesome responsibility that is often taken far too lightly. The improper use of authority is not much different from the careless handling of toxic waste. Transparency and accountability may help prevent the abuses common to hierarchies, but positions of power often allow their holders to dodge accountability and cloud transparency.

As with innovation and tradition, some compromise must be struck between participation, autonomy and hierarchical control. Societies can limit the amount of authority granted to only that which is needed to perform a job. Systems of checks and balances may be employed. If political and/or economic organizations of size are going to exist, then some form of hierarchy may be necessary, but it should be limited to such a degree that it has no more authority than is needed to fulfill its function. How to define and make operative concepts like transparency, accountability, and limitations to authority then become the next questions one would start thinking about in trying to address these matters.

19. SOME SUGGESTIONS IN POLITICAL ECONOMIC THOUGHT

Political economics represents the category of philosophical inquiry that deals with societies' organizational and economic activities. Like our other areas of inquiry, it involves standards of workability, consistency, evidence, values, and free will.

Although political economics involves the same fallibilities as other types of beliefs, we can tentatively posit some working beliefs. Political economics in full only comes into play when (1) a society is advanced enough to have excess resources after all the basic survival needs have been met and (2) has some degree of choice as to what to do with those resources. When these conditions have been met, societies can start selecting between various goals as long as they respect things like the moral minimums. Beyond that, most societies will make additional decisions based on their particular circumstances though there may not always be agreement on which goals to accept or prioritize and these decisions may always be in flux.

The complexity of the world makes it almost impossible to test political economics on the criterion of "workability." So many variables contribute to the failure or success of a society that it's almost impossible to tell what role political and economic choices have played. But certain values seem to increase the chances of societal success. One of these is an open society, one which values innovation. A society that devotes resources to learning without being fearful of change is one that, for example, might have ideas about what to do when rats carrying the plague debark from ships from the Mediterranean.

Another of these is values is a careful concern for hierarchy. Unless the political system to be used is fully inclusive in requiring something like fully informed, un-coerced, and unanimous consent—and this consent can be completely retracted at any moment—one or more individuals is probably wielding more power than others. This may well be the point of political organization; to allow for the making of decisions that direct action collectively toward goals or ends. But in the end it still allows one person or an oligarchy to issue orders and expect compliance to their commands, within the limits of their authority, and in the absence of compliance impose penalties or deny benefits. This can even lead to the highly undesirable situation of one person—a dictator—having authority over the life and autonomy of others.

Most modern societies have recognized the need for compromise in these areas. Unbridled innovation can led to dangerous experimentation, and a total lack of hierarchy may well lead to anarchy. The type of analysis we use here for open societies and hierarchy can be applied to other ideas for political and economic organization as well, to determine their feasibility. With this approach, we can sort through better and worse suggestions for political and economic organizations and at least get a good idea of the guts or foundations of our justifications for such social arrangements.

A great deal more has been said and needs to be said about these and related topics but I wanted to include at least a short discussion of political and bit of economic thought as it helps demonstrate how layers of the jigsaw sphere can inter-relate and depend on upon on another to be understood and justified. If what works is our criteria for deciding between intellectual options then this criteria is applicable in what we think about any subject, the very point of developing a criteria by which beliefs are evaluated. If beliefs need to be consistent, then our views about ethics cannot be at variance with our beliefs about what is and what is not a good society.

V

Conclusion: From Faith to Philosophy

20. SELF-MAPPING ROBOTS

When you view humanity as intelligent and occasionally educated monkey (or variety of ape—the "Naked Ape," as Desmond Morris would have it), some odd habits become apparent. Among these is the tendency for these monkeys to think in terms of knowledge. While I don't much doubt that animals can have, through memory, experience, reason, and perhaps inherited memories, a bit of understanding of their surrounding environment, at least in terms of their wants and needs, I don't think they are in position to know very much for certain.

Humans have devised very detailed explanations of themselves and their surroundings. Inquiry may be part of human-primate instinct or impulse, but this inquiry needs to be informed by the limits that seemingly exist for the inquirer. Claiming certainty for our beliefs about matters, be them ethical or otherwise, fails to acknowledge the limits of just who is asking and answering these questions. There are better and worse beliefs, as discussed throughout this book, but we cannot claim to possess much that counts as knowledge. Systems of thought that attempt to bring the concept of certainty into play will usually suffer as explanations.

When it comes to ethics, this lack of certainty comes into play. Both fallible ethical realism and fallible ethical non-realism are possible lines of thought in ethics that don't seem to get one into impossible intellectual troubles. Infallible ethical realism I don't think possible as I don't think primates are very often infallible about reality. Infallible ethical non-realism is problematic, however, for the same and different reasons.

Insofar as ethics is a judgment to value life and is not a statement of fact or reality, one might think it possible for this understanding to render certainty or something very close to certainty in values. This is the certainty that comes with fiction in that I can be certain, or very, very close to certain, that Sherlock Holmes lived at 22B Baker Street and not 22A. If I am ever in doubt I can simply consult the stories on Holmes. Or, in the case of ethics, if as part of my choice to value life I have decided dishonesty is wrong, I can be certain or very, very close to certain that I should discard a temptation to deceive.

There are two issues to keep in mind here; the first is that of making a choice: deciding to value life, to act ethically. The choice here is made or not made but this choice is not a matter of choosing the true or the false. It is merely choosing one path over another, there is nothing to be infallible about. Thus infallible ethical non-realism, at least in regards to this first decision, is not viable, as there is ultimately nothing to be right or wrong about. Ethics is a matter of choice and judgment, where terms like better, worse, best, and worst are in application, not terms like true and false.

The second issue that infallible ethical non-realism runs across is a similar problem to that of infallible ethical realism in that we can never be quite sure we have found the best method of valuing life. To value a life is not to solely impose our sense of value on it, as Kant notes; we need to respect life as an end and never as a means only. To value life is to try to understand it, to see what makes it grow and flourish or at least to keep it out of harm's way as much as possible. The best or better methods of doing this are not always clear and it is here that our limitations come into play again. We are limited inquirers, not beings marching quickly toward omniscience.

Nietzsche and Self-Mapping Machines

The one area of certainty for us is our own self-awareness. Part I of this book makes the case for the firm foundation for this certainty. But not every philosopher agrees. One of the critics of this truth in self-awareness was Friedrich Nietzsche, a nineteenth-century philosopher who addresses what he sees as a problem with being certain of our self-awareness in his book *Beyond Good and Evil*. I will quote him at length here:

> There are still some harmless self-observers who believe that there are "immediate certainties"; for example, "I think" or as the superstition of Schopenhauer put it, "I will"; as though knowledge here got hold of its object purely and nakedly as "the thing in itself," without any falsification on the part of either the subject or object. But that "immediate certainty," as well as "absolute knowledge" and the thing in itself, involve a *contradicitio in adjecto*

> (contradiction between the noun and the adjective.) I shall repeat it a hundred times: we really ought to free ourselves of the seduction of words.
>
> Let the people suppose that knowledge means knowing things entirely; the philosopher must say to himself: When I analyze the process expressed in the sentence, "I think," I find a whole series of daring assertions, what would be difficult, perhaps impossible, to prove, for example that it is I who think, that there must be an operation of the part of being who is thought of as a cause, that there is an "ego," and finally, that it is already determined what is being designated by thinking—that I know what thinking is. For if I had not already decided within myself what it is, by what standard could I determine within myself what it is. In short, the assertion "I think" assumes that I compare my state at the present moment with other states of myself which I know, in order to determine what it is; on account of this retrospective connection with further "knowledge," it has, at any rate, no immediate certainty for me.
>
> In place of the "immediate certainty" in which the people may believe in the case at hand, the philosopher thus finds a series of metaphysical questions presented to him, truly searching questions of the intellect; to wit: "From where do I get the concept of thinking? Why do I believe in cause and effect? What gives me the right to speak of an ego, and even as an ego as cause, and finally as the cause of thought?" Whoever ventures to answer these metaphysical questions at once by an appeal to a sort of intuitive perception—like the person who says, "I think, and know that this, at least, is true, actual and certain"—will encounter a smile and two question marks from a philosopher nowadays. "Sir," the philosopher will perhaps give him to understand, "it is improbable that you are not mistaken; but why insist on the truth?"

I was aware of this critique by Nietzsche when I wrote my first book but did not include it for various reasons. I would like to discuss it now and use it in an attempt to shed light on the evidence that supports my claim to knowledge of self-awareness, or "truth" as Nietzsche would have it.

I would like to contrast the above, very quickly, with the description of the process I provided in chapter eight of my first book; it is provided below to save the reader troubles . . .

> It appears to me that the strength of Descartes's proof of his own existence hinges upon three things. It hinges upon a self-evident foundation, the self-awareness of a perception and upon a very tight chain of reasoning. One might re-phrase Descartes' proof, in the light of the above, as follows:
>
> 1. The experience of a perception is only possible if something exists which experiences the perception.
> 2. I, Rene Descartes, am currently experiencing a perception.
> 3. I, Rene Descartes, must exist."

The above is not just an immediate perception, is not purely a trick of grammar. Grammar is required to state this matter but is not what makes the matter accurate. If I could put my self-awareness for you to see directly into the text I would at this point, but I don't have any idea how to do this outside of words and grammar. This does not mean I do not currently perceive a perception; I alone can be certain of that.

Still there is reason to be wary of grammar or semantics leading philosophy and of using terms that are ill-defined or poorly understood. Nietzsche is seemingly correct to bring these issues into the discussion. Perhaps a rephrasing of the above, wary of grammar/semantics leading philosophy, might work along the lines of "I see mind." If I can show how one might do an adequate job of defining these three terms without a great deal of grammar, I might not be guilty of crossing too many swords with Nietzsche on this matter.

- "I = will, thought, desire, feeling, bundle of mental experiences."
- "See = awareness of something, mental experience of something"
- "Mind = mental experience"
- "I see mind = bundle of mental experiences has mental experience of mental experience"

I am not sure how much point there is to continuing the above in terms of this text, though it is fun to write. The point is that the proof of one's self-awareness rests in the self-awareness alone. Self-awareness, by and of itself, is enough to give certainty; the proof does not lie in words and grammar.

I also think Nietzsche is correct to note that just the phrase "I think . . ." brings a great deal of baggage with it. We do need to have some idea of what is intended by these terms and their definitions. Once constructed and construed, however, his concerns can then be addressed and matters modified or changed as best seems to fit. Over time, seemingly preferable definitions and concepts can be worked out such that this critique loses much of its bite.

As a final note, there are also many who deny mind by believing that only matter is real, who may well think I am mistaken on this point of self-awareness. However, since my evidence for my mind is greater than the evidence of their existence, it would seem that I should not take them too seriously. After all, I know I exist but the rest of my beliefs are fallible. Perhaps these mindless things are reporting on themselves, much like a robot might draw a diagram of itself without being conscious. Robots merely following a self-mapping program, but they are not reporting on me. Of this I am certain.

21. THE PROBLEM WITH FAITH: THE METAPHOR OF THE LIBRARY

Imagine walking into a library with 50,000 books on philosophy, law, religion, science, theology—the great matters of humanity, if you will allow it. Now imagine plucking one of these books randomly from the shelf, without studying or even reading the titles of the other books, and saying to yourself, "this book is true and it is completely true; if any of these other books disagree with it then they are false."

How would you know if it was better than the others or that it was completely true? You could not know this as it is not possible to know this from your method. If you read at length in the library and talked to people who have also read at the library it would seemingly be possible, in time, to develop a much better opinion of the better or best books at the library. This, however, is because you are using a good method of inquiry, a method that will help you sort arbitrary from non-arbitrary beliefs about the books.

It is hard to see how accepting beliefs on faith is different from randomly plucking the book from the shelf in the story above. It is hard to see how it is not accepting a belief for arbitrary reasons. It is difficult to see how the statement "I believe x" is made stronger, more believable, by "I believe x because I have faith in x." This second statement may tell others one has a strong personal conviction about the matter but it does not seem to give any reason to think "x" is more probable or accurate than any other belief. Faith is not like evidence or consistency and it does no work in terms of giving reason to think something accurate; at best it is an indicator of the degree to which someone thinks something to be true.

I think this becomes quite clear if you distinguish between trust and faith. Trust is more believing without enough evidence to make a conclusive demonstration of what you believe. It is to go beyond, but not too far beyond, the boundaries of what is demonstrable. If I believe my bank account is safe at the moment, even though I have not just checked it today or in the last few moments, there is a little bit of trust involved. This trust is based on the bank's good conduct with the account in the past and similar reports from others about its conduct, but belief in the safety of my money has a bit of trust in it. Similarly, if I leave the room during an exam there is a least a bit of trust on my part that the students will not cheat; if I think the students are likely to cheat in my absence, this act of trust becomes more an act of faith.

Faith, at least how it is bandied about in some circles, is having no evidence, next to no evidence, or even contradictory evidence but still determining that something is true or false, still claiming knowledge of the matter. It is to decide a question or issue without respect for reason or the evidence and to confidently call it something we know to be true. It is to walk into the library above and select one book at random and call it true. It is one thing to test, to spend the time necessary to become familiar with the library, and then make a determination on the better books; it is another thing entirely to select a text without effort and then decide to believe it.

Concerns about consistency also immediately begin to raise their heads when you start discussing faith. Consistency seemingly demands that two opposing and contradictory beliefs cannot both be true. The Islamic view that Jesus was a prophet and not the son of God cannot be combined with the Christian view of Jesus being the son of God. Faith can justify both Christianity and Islam on this point and yet consistency tells us that at least one must be false.

The Catholics include books in their Bible that the Protestants exclude from their Bible. If I have faith that the Catholic Bible is the complete and total word of God and you have faith that the Protestant Bible is the complete and total word of God, are we both correct? This would seem to be impossible. The Bibles are different and cannot both, in reality, be the complete and total word of God. It is possible that neither of them is the complete and total word of God, or that one of them might fit the bill, but it is not possible both are the complete and total word of God. At least one, if not both, must be wrong, and faith cannot solve this problem.

I have described faith as an arbitrary method of forming beliefs. I am aware that such a description may cause discomfort. There are, however, ethical concerns with the employment of faith if the employment of this faith affects others. It might be worthwhile to compare the use of faith to smoking cigarettes; not only is it bad for you, it is bad for those around you as well.

Unless one is shipwrecked on a deserted island, becomes a hermit, or in some other way manages to completely isolate one's self from everyone else, it is hard to not have an impact on others. What and why we believe has a strong influence on how we live, our quality and type of life, how we behave towards others, and so on. To go not only beyond the evidence, but far beyond the evidence, in matters of what we think and believe and then tell others to follow our lead is to put both ourselves and them at risk.

We might live in a better world if it was a more forgiving one. Mistakes in interacting with nature and humanity are many times punished and often punished swiftly. Attempting to fashion reasonably accurate beliefs is not just about achieving a certain intellectual standard of thought or satisfaction. This is not just about truth for the sake of truth; there are other issues at play as well. Accurate beliefs are not only intellectually preferable, they can also be a matter of life or death, war or peace, prosperity or poverty, and they can touch nearly every aspect of our existence.

Additionally, if we form some beliefs about matters in an arbitrary fashion we also run the very real risk of making arbitrary ethical judgments when no such thing was seemingly necessary. If a book we believe for arbitrary reasons tells us that a certain group of people is evil (homosexuals, overtly sexual women, non-believers, believers of a different faith, etc.) when they are not bad, really horrible things can and do happen to other people. Faith poses dangers to us, our communities, and other communities as well. Furthermore when such a concept is tied to significant destructive power, it can endanger whole nations if not the entire species.

Faith is not just the supplying of simple answers to complex questions. It is very dangerous and one of humanity's great follies. To think one can really find significant solutions to problems and questions by closing one's eyes and guessing does not seem possible. The old adage "if something is worth doing it is worth doing well" applies to developing one's beliefs as much as to craftsmanship, cooking, or matters of personal finance.

While it seems odd to think anyone would voluntarily accept arbitrary beliefs, this becomes quite possible when you confuse good and bad reasons for why you believe something. Hopes and desires can be very strong. As Aristotle notes in his *Nichomachean Ethics*, we don't blame others for having feelings; what is praiseworthy or shameful depends, however, upon what we do in regard to these feelings, emotions, and desires.

The non-rational elements of the mind may well provide us with a direction or orientation in terms of our interests and goals, but beyond perhaps playing the role of a compass they have little application in these matters. One may want to ultimately head north and the compass can point out which way is north, but the best route is not determined by the compass. Traveling north from one's current location may well require a boat. Heading south and then west before going north may well be the best option if one has only a car. As Plato has noted, the rational or reasoning side of the mind seems very well-suited to making determinations about the best ways to go about this or that, of finding the best path north.

Faith is thus more a denial of a significant role for thought, reason, or evidence in constructing or evaluating our beliefs. "Believe this, don't believe that, don't ask questions, just accept my word as truth, and whatever you do don't seriously think about it or ultimately doubt it." Indeed it seems hard not to see such efforts to minimize or eliminate independent thought about the most important questions as a product of the fear of change and fear of the unknown. In my first book, *Some Thoughts on Thinking*, I take up the question of trying to distinguish between science, philosophy, theology, and religion where attempts to understand the divine are distinguished from making assumptions about important matters. Others, as well, have taken up this theme and as I have stated, my view is not much different from Clifford's in the first part to this three-part essay *The Ethics of Belief*. An interested reader is recommended to take up further discussion of the matter there.

To make a quick point of clarification, faith does not play into matters of ethical judgment in the system I have outlined earlier. When one chooses to value life or to live ethically, one is not making an epistemic, evidential, or rational determination. Evidence and reasoning are not in application. This is not a matter that can be settled by an appeal to evidence and logic. This is a choice, a judgment call: I choose to pursue and promote life or I do not. Ethics, in this setting, is more a matter of making or not making a direct mental determination; it is not something that is true or false. It can be true or false that you have or have not made this determination but the determination itself is a non-evidential matter until it is finally made. Once you make the decision to be ethical, factual concerns about how to properly treat others become highly relevant, but they are not relevant in the initial determination of whether or not to be ethical, which is the beginning of ethics.

22. THE START OF A THEOLOGY: TWIGTI

It seems to take human beings a very short time on Earth to realize that we aren't omnipotent. We often don't get what we want and do get what we don't want. The world fails to obey our wishes. It seems to follows that there is at least one thing, if not many, many things, that have the power to thwart my will, to make me less comfortable than I would otherwise choose to be. This thing or things, being or beings, is what I call TWIGTI: That Which Is Greater Than I.

By definition TWIGTI has the potential for greater influence in my life than I do. But what else might we be able to say about it? There are three general perspectives on the nature of TWIGTI proposed through history: that it is benevolent, caring, or basically good in nature; that it is malevolent, of ill-intent, or basically evil in nature; or that it is neutral, uncaring, unaware of us, or uninterested. Christianity and Plato both posit that TWIGTI is benevolent, though for Plato it is not conscious, not something or someone you can talk to, and for Christians it is conscious and one can speak with it. Zarathustra and the Maccabees believed the TWIGTI to be at least partly malevolent and saw nature divided into good and evil sides that are at war with each other.

My own journey of developing working beliefs led me to favor the view that the TWIGTI is neutral and quite possibly even uncaring: it is neither for me nor against me. This can be a difficult conclusion for someone raised in a faith tradition to accept, so some years ago, as a thought experiment, I started working on a modified Protestant theology. I wanted to see if one could construct a working belief on the benevolence of TWIGTI in line with the Christian tradition that did not make use of any assumptions or faith-based reasoning. I use the term "theology" deliberately, for theology is a thought process regarding God, whereas "religion" is the practice of faith.

Part of the result of my efforts was the invention of what I call "The Gospel of Saint Simon." My fictional story is rooted in historical fact. In the fourth century AD, in North Africa there were a number of people who renounced human society and went to live in the desert in an attempt to achieve greater spiritual insight. Among these desert dwellers was Simeon the Pillar Saint, a man who lived on top of ruined pillar for the better part of his adult life.

The Gospel According to Simon

The rejection of the human body is something fairly unnatural and thus its very act brings a great deal of attention. Simon the Billboard Saint, as I call him, used the same strategy to great effect on a coastal highway in Texas. His father's church had rented a billboard and Simon, after finishing two years of college had built a small elevated platform on its front and now sat in peaceful testimony to his beliefs, which appeared on the sign beside him. The billboard read:

THE GOSPEL ACCORDING TO SIMON:

1. "This is my command, Love each other."
2. "You have heard it said, Love your neighbor and hate your enemies. But I tell you: Love your enemies."
3. "Love your enemies, do good to those that hate you."
4. "Blessed are those who hunger and thirst for righteousness . . . Blessed are the merciful . . . Blessed are the peacemakers.
5. "The good man brings out the good stored up in his heart, and the evil man brings evil things out of the evil stored up in his heart."
6. "Do not murder, do not commit adultery, do not steal, do not give false testimony, honor your father and your mother . . . love your neighbor as yourself."
7. "What good is it for a man to gain the whole world and yet forfeit his very self?"
8. "Be on your guard against all kinds of greed; a man's life does not consist in the abundance of possessions."
9. "Do not store for yourselves treasures . . . where moth and rust destroy and where thieves break in and steal . . . for where your treasure is, there you heart will be also."
10. "Why do you look at the speck of sawdust in your brother's eye and pay no attention to the plank in your own eye? How can you say to your brother, 'Brother, let me take the speck out of your eye' when you fail to see the plank in your own eye?"
11. "Everyone who hears these words of mine and puts them into practice is like a wise man . . . but everyone who hears these words of mine and does not put them into practice is like a foolish man."
12. "Wisdom is proved right by her actions."

This is a bit much to take in the first time you see the sign as Simon himself draws attention but with multiple exposures or taking the time to stop, read or take a picture the whole scene unfolds. After the checking the situation out a few times I parked my car on the side of the road, called out to him and asked if I might climb the ladder to speak with him.

Simon was quite friendly for one who lived such an austere lifestyle, but one would occasionally get a glimpse of its' impact when he would fall silent for minutes at a time before returning to the conversation. I had recognized some of the sayings printed on the billboard as quotes from the New Testament but did not recognize the terms "The Gospel of Simon." Matters became a little clearer when he told me his name was Simon but I still did not understand the meaning of the phrase and after the introductions decided to ask directly about it.

"Do you mind if I ask you a question?"

"Nope, go right ahead."

"I know that gospel means "good news," but I have never heard of The Gospel of Simon. What is that?"

"It is the Bible I edited."

"The Bible you edited!?"

This last exclamation brought a bit of smile to his face. He drew a deep breath as if to begin speaking at length and then proceeded to do so . . .

"The Catholic Bible is longer, contains more books, than the Protestant bible. The Protestants will sometimes refer to these other or missing materials as 'the hidden books' or the Apocrypha. From one point of view, given that the Protestants come after and broke-away from the Catholic Church, one could say they took scissors to the Catholic Bible and cut away what they did not like. The Protestants claim that the omitted books do not belong for various reasons, and the Catholics will claim that they do belong for various reasons. One example in these exchanges should suffice to show the state of this debate; the Protestants claim, among other things, that the hidden books did not generate the same religious, poetic, or prophetic feelings as the other books they accept . . ."

I stopped Simon with my hand at this point. "I am not sure what this disagreement between the Catholics and the Protestants has to do with you and your sign."

He slightly smiled once again. "Let's just put it this way: What is the word of God and what is not the word of God, is not at all clear or easy to determine."

"I still don't see the connection."

At this point Simon went into one of his silent modes for a few minutes before saying, "The Jefferson Bible, compiled by Thomas Jefferson, one of our early presidents, is literally a cut and pasted version of the four gospels; Jefferson decided what stayed in, what was taken out, and what order it was presented in. As Jefferson remarks himself, the words of Jesus were written down by poorly lettered men long after Jesus had died. Easy to make mistakes in what was said and to confuse things quite a bit."

"So," I said slowly as I put it together, "you think what is and what is not the word of God is hard to determine so you took out what did not think belonged in the text?"

Another long spell of thought, as Simon seemed to be concentrating on another problem. Finally he spoke: "Something like that. I had a method, though; I focused on the words of Jesus that concentrated on conduct between people. How people should treat one another, how we should get along. This to me seems the more important matter."

This gave me a bit of pause before I asked "But what about a person's relationship to God? Isn't this a big part of what the Christian religion is about, at least as I understand it?"

"It is hard to imagine a good father being more concerned about your love for him than for his love for you and your life as you go through it. It would be an odd father that said 'as long as you confide in me and tell me you love me, you can do what you want to your brothers, sisters, friends and strangers.'"

I thought this a good point and it took me a moment to blurt out "But what about doing both?"

This brought a short spell upon Simon. "How and in what fashion one can develop a relationship with God is not at all clear. Smiles and tears are not so hard to distinguish."

"Thus," I said once again slowly, "you have edited the Bible to focus on people's treatment of other people and dropped the rest because it is too deep?"

Another, but much longer, silent spell ensued. Then Simon continued: "It is too deep as it is too obscure unless you have mastered something like the ethics on the sign and have decided to dedicate oneself to the search. As Protagoras, an ancient Greek thinker remarked, 'Concerning the gods . . . many things hinder certainty—the obscurity of the matter and the shortness of man's life.' What is and what is not the word of God and how one develops a relationship with this totality is not at all clear. To get concerned with miracles and creation stories or promises of eternal life is to miss the point. It just makes little sense to miss the teachings of Jesus because one gets caught up the stories about Christ. How to behave is more important than any concern about the dead rising from the grave and your place in paradise. Jefferson's Bible and my own Gospel distill an ethic of Jesus from the stories about Christ, leaving out other matters that distract from the ethical message."

The ladder was starting to get uncomfortable, but I wanted some more answers so I decided to stick it out for a little longer. I reopened the conversation politely with "You have some good one-liners. I really liked 'Smiles and tears are not so hard to distinguish.' Once again, where did you get permission, the authority, to do all of this?"

This brought a laugh and he shyly quipped, "I am self-appointed." He then fell into another of his silences before he said quietly, "I take this stuff very seriously. In a marketplace of ideas each participant is allowed to put his ideas out for display for those who care to take a look. It is not unheard of to think ethics a good and first step in the study of things. Learning to live ethically and honestly prepare you to think ethically and honestly about the greater matters. If you approach them without these preparations, you are much more apt to see what you want to see and miss seeing things altogether." He then added with a little smile, "In addition to becoming a jerk."

Simon then continued very earnestly. "My gospel does not require faith, as faith is an extremely dangerous path for thought. An ethic if lived can prove itself to those who live it; no act of faith is required. There is no need to guess about the great matters when it is possible to demonstrate the important things to yourself through your own efforts. I do not ask people to believe me; I ask them to believe themselves."

This brought a pause and long silence on myself before I asked, "Lots of people rely upon faith for their daily lives. Do you really think it that foolish?"

"Yes." After a short silence he added, "I don't think they use it in their daily lives at all in fact. Very few people, if any, pick their spouses or friends using faith; one does not randomly open the phone-book, point to a name, and then say this person is a good auto mechanic for faith has made it true. We don't use faith, wild guesses, in daily life—only to avoid grappling with the great issues."

"So faith is used only matters we do not feel comfortable addressing?"

"Exactly."

"What about trust?"

"Trust is different from faith. I may trust a friend because I have known him for years and he has proved true and reliable. Trust is a matter of having some evidence but not enough to be sure; faith is having no evidence and being confident. For my gospel trust is not even required as you can check the matter out for yourself."

"What about hope?"

"Hope is also different from faith and trust. Hope is wanting something to be true, wanting something to happen. One can hope and know there is little chance of good news. One can even hope when there seems no chance, but this is different from believing one's hope to be true without any reason for thinking it to be true. Faith can allow full, complete, and total belief in something that has no chance of being true, as faith does not take reasons and evidence into considerations in passing its judgments. Trust and hope are not opposed to reason and evidence. Trust and hope exist within the boundaries of reason and evidence; faith does not. Hope and trust are thus good things, if kept inside the boundaries of reason and evidence. It is hard to see how one keeps faith inside boundaries it does not recognize."

I thought about this for minute. "Could anyone do the same thing you have done? Can I write my own gospel?"

"Yes, I would encourage that. I encourage taking these matters seriously and engaging in them in such a fashion. Indeed what I have done is only to make explicit a process that has been implicitly in operation in Christianity from its very beginning. What is and what is not the word of God is very hard to determine, and thus attempts to revise the Bible occur from time to time with things being added or subtracted. Taking the time to work out what you think is worth the effort if you would like to better understand these matters. I advise one to begin with ethics for the reasons I mentioned earlier, but that is up to you. It seems odd to believe but to not to take the time to learn about that which one claims to believe. Indeed, to what degree can one believe something if one does not understand it? If I simply learn a phrase in a foreign language, without learning that language or the meaning of the phrase, and I repeat it by heart and believe it on faith, in what sense do I understand the phrase?"

This hit a little too close to home and I was really getting tired of standing on the ladder so I decided to ask a final question as I started moving down the ladder.

"Do you have any good stories from your seat up here?"

Simon smiled and said a local preacher had come by and complained that Simon was creating "Refrigerator Christianity," as one could put his entire Bible easily on piece of paper on the fridge. He also mentioned that some women would occasionally reveal their upper halves as they passed by in cars and that this was a nice perk. This got a quick chuckle and I then thanked Simon for the conversation and said the ladder was getting tiresome. Simon nodded and thanked me for stopping by as well. I waved good-bye to Simon from the car, he waved back and then I tucked this into a corner in the mind until a few minutes ago.

23. EPILOGUE: MY JOURNEY FROM FAITH TO PHILOSOPHY

I began this book with a preface that described my religious upbringing, which culminated in a crisis of belief. That crisis led me to philosophy, to the search for a more solid foundation for my beliefs which I have hopefully done a good job replicating here. Simon, the Pillar Saint, provided an example of how one might use these lessons in constructing a theology instead of the philosophical system previously out-lined. We thus have two examples of attempting to use honest inquiry to render viable explanations of our experiences. Before we finish, however, I would like to directly discuss how these various lessons overlap into forming a system of thought.

Philosophy is often divided into five topics or categories: epistemology, metaphysics, ethics, political economics, and aesthetics. This work has addressed the first four of these in the course of its effort. Part I focused on epistemology, the study of knowledge—how we can know or justify things. Part II considered metaphysics, the study of what is believed to be real, questions of matter, mind, soul, and the freedom of the will. Part III delved into ethics, the consideration of right and wrong behavior. This fourth part added some thoughts on human organization or the some basic points to think about when trying to do political economics. Epistemology, metaphysics, ethics, and political economics all interrelate in a very interesting and logical fashion. For instance, what is thought to be a good society depends upon what one thinks is proper or ethical. If one is a staunch proponent of human rights then societies that lack commitments to human rights may well be seen as wrong-headed. What one thinks is good or ethical depends on what one thinks to be real, one's metaphysical beliefs. What one thinks is real is tied in with epistemology, the way we can know or justify things.

To say this all another way, what is thought to be real depends on what one is prepared to count as reasoning and evidence. What is thought to be good or ethical is dependent on what one thinks to be real and the better forms of political and economic arrangement are dependent upon what is considered right or wrong. Like in a mobile, if you touch one of the pieces they all move, as the demands of consistency run throughout.

Christian thought can afford a very good example of these inter-relationships and it has the added advantage of being a point of view many are probably already familiar with. I am not trying to impart any given view on any individual with these thoughts so I will consider this "my construction" for the sake of simplicity even though this may well reflect the thoughts of others in some or many respects. It is not uncommon for faith to be considered the ultimate epistemology, the path to knowledge of God's existence. That faith gives one reason to think God is real, the basis of Christian metaphysics. Faith leads to God, God leads to Faith. Faith/God then directs one to the Holy Scriptures or the Bible and the Bible explains the will of God. Reality is God-reality; reality is God-created, and it is composed of both spiritual and material forces. Humans have both a spiritual and material existence where the spirit is tempted by the body to sin or to turn away from God.

In this traditional form of Christianity, a good person is one who has faith, studies the Bible, and tries their best to live within the guidelines of the scriptures. Political economics is more difficult to derive from Christian thought, as the interpretation of scripture on political and economic matters has varied greatly over the years. Christianity, as Huston Smith observes, more grafts itself, like a vine, upon pre-existing political economic structures. While Christians frequently want a say in government, rarely is political and economic life utterly subsumed within the Christian church. One could argue, however, that Christian political economics should focus on mirroring heaven on earth as much as possible.

In short, the four categories of philosophy are dealt with in traditional Christianity in the following way:

- Epistemology: Knowledge of God ensures faith, while faith ensures knowledge of God
- Metaphysics: Faith confirms the reality of God, souls, matter, and free will
- Ethics: The values of good and evil can be discerned from the Bible
- Political Economics: Political and economic activity should mirror the organization and values of heaven on Earth

Although devout believers accept these things on faith, philosophy requires looking over these statements and evaluating them for workability and internal consistency. My own philosophical journey led me to conclude that the above is too poorly constructed. I would probably start by stating that proving God with faith and faith with God is too circular, but the statements also fail other requirements of good thought discussed throughout this text.

Another example of system building is possible if we were to build a system of thought out of Simon the Billboard Saint's gospel. Simon's thought process begins with ethics on the grounds that one needs the discipline that ethics demands to face questions in philosophy and theology honestly. Epistemology is then, for Simon, a matter of honest inquiry, an honest inquiry which then leads on to an understanding of Christ's revelation. This Christian revelation provides the basis for a Christian metaphysic or a God-reality, and a God-reality gives one a further foundation for ethics. Simon, like many Christian saints, does not address political economics.

In a similar fashion philosophy allows us to construct a non-arbitrary foundation for our beliefs. It begins with self-awareness and then proceeds to use the demands of workability and consistency to justify the statement of some tentative working beliefs. Among the beliefs so justified is the belief that there is both mind and matter, that we have freedom in regard to our will, and an ethics based on robustly valuing life fits the world better than the belief in an objective, universal set of ethics. We are then left with a fallible but not hopeless basis for working out our views about political economics.

That basis will be continually subject to review. We should constantly ask ourselves where the weak points in our system of thought is, where it might go wrong. For instance, a good deal of the epistemic side of this work has been based around our awareness of our own thoughts and the foundation this gives to the rest of one's beliefs. If this foundation is found to be mistaken, misconceived or just down right wrong that which has been built upon it will suffer as explanations. If consistency is found to be a false idol, it is lost as one of the criteria by which I suggested we use to sort through various explanations.

Beyond the base certainty of our own self-awareness, beliefs are matters of probability, justification, and warrant, not a matter of knowledge. As a consequence of this approach we must be ready to change or modify our beliefs, our thoughts, if they can be made to better fit or describe our experiences. By not overcommitting to any given belief it is possible to remain flexible in regard to any other belief, to be prepared to change beliefs if matters warrant a change. The same is true of our beliefs regarding mind and body, free will or non-realistic value systems. Any system must understand humanity as fallible in nearly every matter. After one has constructed in philosophy it is quite common to turn to the deconstruction of the same. A never-ending process of refinement perhaps, but unless one has learned everything there is more room to grow and more beliefs to be rethought.

Bibliography

I never would have thought such an introduction to a bibliography would be necessary but there are a number of concerns that make this a necessity. The first is that I was living abroad, in the Czech Republic, when the raw material for this book was written. I had left the United States in December of 1999 and moved to Prague, the capital of the Czech Republic. As I was planning on being gone a long time, and perhaps not returning to live in the United States, I took my extensive library with me. A collection that I had started building with my first college textbooks and had continued to build ever since, every major and most of the minor works in Western philosophy was either there in full or at least represented in an encyclopedia, anthology, etc. The books were like an extension of me, another appendage, my most valued and prized possessions as I had never been married and have no children and one does not possess one's parents, spouse, children, relatives or siblings in any case.

All told the collection weighed 1,200 pounds or so when I tried to ship it back to the US seven years later. My father had developed a rare cancer; I had returned home to help out with the family farm and started teaching again at some local universities. Of the 23 postal shipping bags sent from Prague, each of which weighed about 55 pounds, only eight arrived back in the US. I had no problem getting the whole collection to the Czech Republic, but getting my intact library back to the US proved impossible.

I was told by the Czech Postal Service that it might take up to a year to ship all these bags and they might come in separate groups. The bags were in effect flying stand-by and would be shipped when there was room. Thus when only 8 of the 23 bags arrived initially, I did not worry about it and I let about six months come and go with only a single phone call to the post office that confirmed that there was nothing I could do but wait. This single confirming phone call was made in the third month since the books were placed in the mail. Subsequently there might still have been time to save the books if action had been under-taken by the post office at that time. I was told to wait by a post office that was preparing to sell my books for pennies on the dollar as lost mail; presumably one hand did not know what the other was doing.

When I began following up with US postal service in earnest, (six months after they were originally mailed and two months or so after they were sold at a lost mail auction in Atlanta, Georgia), I was told I had to start the complaint process in the postal office from which I mailed the bags, back in the Czech Republic. The Czechs, as per their stated policy, would not start an investigation until a year had passed. A mad scramble now ensues on my part, I am calling anyone I can think of who might be able to remotely help. Finally by talking to a very helpful agent of the German airline Lufthansa, the airline with whom the bags were shipped, I was able to determine that all the bags had arrived in Newark, New Jersey and that the missing bags had been shipped to the lost mail facility in Atlanta, Georgia. When I contacted the lost mail facility I learned that my books had already been sold as lost mail is moved out fairly quickly, four months or so after it gets lost. By the time I had started looking for the lost books in earnest, they had already been sold. It was never really possible to use the postal system to track the books before they were gone.

The story continues as I talk to attorneys and try to get the US government's permission to sue it. At the end of the day, however, the books were lost and in short, I don't really care if the US postal system is dissolved tomorrow. Thus when I wrote the first drafts of this text I had my full library and now when I turn to assemble the bibliography only remnants are left of it. I have replaced some of the missing texts but it is no longer possible to be sure that I have included every text that I originally read or employed in my efforts. A terrible loss for me personally but I try to keep this in perspective as other have suffered far worse than the loss of a personal library. Nonetheless as I look at my books arranged around the walls there are no doubts that I have forgotten a large number of my old friends in this bibliography.

PART ONE

Augustine, "The City of God," translated by Marcus Dods, D.D., Hendrickson Publishers, 2013. (Book XI, 26, in particular.)
Bergmann, Moor and Nelson, "The Logic Book," Random House, 1980.
Bulfinch, Thomas, "Bulfinch's Mythology," Gramercy Books, 2005.
Copi and Cohen, "Introduction to Logic," Pearson Education, 1998, 11th edition.
Descartes, "Meditations on First Philosophy," translated by Lafleur, Larence, J., MacMillian Publishing, 1989.
Descartes, "Selected Philosophical Writings," translated by John Cottingham, Robert Stoothoff, and Dugold Murdoch, Cambridge University Press, 1989.
Finch, Jonathan, "Some Thoughts on Thinking," University Press of America, 2002.

Bibliography

Haack, Susan, "A Foundherenist Theory of Empirical Justification," appearing in "Theory of Knowledge: Classical and Contemporary Sources," edited by Pojman, L. 2nd edition, Wadsworth, 1998. Reprinted in E. Sosa's and J. Kim's "Epistemology," Blackwell, 1993.

Haack, Susan, "Evidence and Inquiry, Second Expanded Edition," Prometheus Books, 2009.

Kant, Immanuel, "Critique of Pure Reason," translated by Norman Smith, unabridged edition, St Martin's Press, 1965.

Plato, "Plato, the Republic," translated by Richard W. Sterling and William C. Scott, W.W. Norton, 1985. (Book seven in particular.)

Smith, Huston, "The World's Religions," HarperCollins, 1991.

Thayer, H.S., "Pragmatism, the Classical Writings," Hackett Publishing, 1982. Peirce, Charles, "How to Make our Ideas Clear" and "The Fixation of Belief."

PART TWO

Campbell, Keith, "Body and Mind," University of Notre Dame, 1992.
Cornford, Francis, "Before and After Socrates," Cambridge University Press, 1932.
Haack, Susan, "Defending Science, within Reason," Prometheus Books, 2003.
Finch, Jonathan, "Some Thoughts on Thinking," University Press of America, 2002.
Mill, John, "A System of Logic," Longmans, Green, Reader, and Dyer, 1872.
Searle, John, "Mind," Oxford University Press, 2004

PART THREE

Aristotle, "Nicomachean Ethics," translated by Terence Irwin, Hackett Publishing, 1999. Chapter One in particular.

Cohen, Stephen, "The Nature of Moral Reasoning," Oxford University Press, 2004.

Finch, Jonathan, "Some Thoughts on Thinking," University Press of America, 2002.

Hume, David, "A Treatise of Human Nature," Oxford University Press, 2000.

Kant, Immanuel, "Groundwork of the Metaphysic of Morals," translated by H.J. Patton, Haper-Perennial, 2009.

Mill, John, "On Liberty," Oxford University Press, 2008.

Mill, John, "Utilitarianism," Hackett Publishing, 1979.

Nietzsche, Friedrich, "A Genealogy of Morals and Ecce Homo" translated by W. Kaufman, Vintage, 1989.

Nietzsche, Friedrich, "Beyond Good and Evil," translated by W. Kaufman, Vintage Books, 1966.

Nietzsche, Friedrich, "The Birth of Tragedy" and "The Case of Wagner," translated by W. Kaufman, Vintage Books, 1967.

Nietzsche, Friedrich, "Twilight of the Idols" and "The Anti-Christ," translated by R.J. Hollingdale, Penguin Classics, 1987.

Plato, "Plato, the Republic," translated by Richard W. Sterling and William C. Scott, W.W. Norton, 1985. (Book nine in particular.)

Plato, "The Trial and Death of Socrates," translated by G.M.A. Grube, Hackett Publishing, 3rd edition, 2000.

Popper, Karl, "The Open Society and its Enemies, The Spell of Plato," Princeton University Press, 1966.

Rachels, James, "The Elements of Moral Philosophy," McGraw Hill, Fourth Edition, 2003.

PART FOUR

Desmond Morris, "The Naked Ape," Delta, 1999.
Headrick, Daniel, "Technology/ A World History," Oxford University Press, 2009.

Heilbroner, Robert, "The Nature and Logic of Capitalism," W.W. Norton, 1985.
Heilbroner, Robert, "The Worldly Philosophers," Touchstone, Revised Seventh Edition, 1999.
Kant, Immanuel, "Critique of Pure Reason," translated by Norman Smith, unabridged edition, St Martin's Press, 1965.
Lemos, Ramon, "Hobbes and Locke," The University of Georgia Press, 1978.
Locke, John, "The Second Treatise Government," edited by Thomas Pearson, MacMillian, 1952.
Marx, Karl, "The Marx/Engels Reader," edited by Robert Tucker, 2nd edition, W.W. Norton, 1978.
Plato, "Plato, the Republic," translated by Richard W. Sterling and William C. Scott, W.W. Norton, 1985.
Rachels, James, "The Elements of Moral Philosophy," McGraw Hill, Fourth Edition, 2003.
Searle, John, "Construction of Social Reality," Free Press, 1995.

PART FIVE

"Holy Bible," New Kings James Version, Thomas Nelson Bibles, 1982.
"The Catholic Bible," Personal Study Edition, Oxford University Press, 1995.
Aristotle, "Nicomachean Ethics," translated by Terence Irwin, Hackett Publishing, 1999.
Augustine, "On Christian Doctrine," translated by D.W Robertson, Jr., MacMillian, 1958.
Augustine, "The City of God," translated by Marcus Dods, D.D., Hendrickson Publishers, 2013. (Book XI, 26, in particular.)
Burger, A. J. "The Ethics of Belief," CreateSpace Independent Publishing Platform, 2008. The first of the three part essay "The Ethics of Belief" by Clifford, in particular.
Descartes, "Meditations on First Philosophy," translated by Lafleur, Larence, J., MacMillian Publishing, 1989.
Descartes, "Selected Philosophical Writings," translated by John Cottingham, Robert Stoothoff, and Dugold Murdoch, Cambridge University Press, 1989.
Freud, Sigmund, "Moses and Monotheism," Vintage Books, 1967.
Jefferson, Thomas, "The Jefferson Bible," Beacon Press, 1989.
Finch, Jonathan, "Some Thoughts on Thinking," University Press of America, 2002.
Jones, W.T., "The Medieval Mind," Wadsworth, Thomson Learning, 1980.
Nietzsche, Friedrich, "Beyond Good and Evil," translated by W. Kaufman, Vintage Books, 1966.
Shelley, Bruce, "Church History in Plain English," Word Publishing, 1995.
Smith, Huston, "The World's Religions," HarperCollins, 1991.
Thayer, H.S., "Pragmatism, the Classical Writings," Hackett Publishing, 1982. Peirce, Charles, "How to Make our Ideas Clear" and "The Fixation of Belief."

www.ingramcontent.com/pod-product-compliance
Lightning Source LLC
Chambersburg PA
CBHW020754230426
43665CB00009B/588